Stress: the modern sickness

For several years Peter Blythe was a Senior Lecturer in Psychology at a college of education. He has now returned to private practice as a psychotherapist and consultant hypnotist, and in order to establish the Institute of Psychosomatic Therapy. He has lectured extensively to both professional and lay audiences throughout the United Kingdom, Ireland and the United States, and has taught many hundreds of doctors and dentists how to use hypnosis in their practices. He has also held courses for the medical and dental professions on the psychodynamics underlying illnesses. Mr Blythe has made numerous television appearances both here and in America and has written widely on his subjects. He is the author of *Hypnotism: Its Power and Practice*.

Peter Blythe

Stress: The Modern Sickness

originally published as *Stress Disease*

Pan Books
London and Sydney

First published 1973 as *Stress Disease* by Arthur Barker Ltd
This edition published 1975 by
Pan Books Ltd, Cavaye Place, London SW10 9PG
2nd printing 1976
© Peter Blythe 1973
ISBN 0 330 23404 7
Printed in Great Britain by
Cox & Wyman Ltd, London, Reading and Fakenham

Contents

This book is dedicated to the one person who, more than anyone else, made it possible

Acknowledgements

I wish to acknowledge the help given to me by Dr Gotthard Booth of New York City, Dr Leonard M. Cohen of Kingsville, Texas, Mr Sydney Rose-Neil of the Acupuncture Association, Colonel Marcus McCausland of the 'Health for a New Era' Foundation, Bill Grossman of Kaleidoscope, G. Seaborne-Jones, David McGlown, Ian Urquhart, Paul Atherton, Dr Rachel Pinney, Mrs B. Wade, The National Federation of Spiritual Healers, Mrs J. Singleton, Brother Mandus of the Divine Healing Fellowship, M. A. Mirza, and many others.

Nor would the book have been possible without the many people I have seen over the years, and I hope they have derived some benefit from the time we spent together.

Preface

When I told various friends that I was planning to write a book about *stress* they were very enthusiastic and encouraged me by saying, 'It's about time, because it is affecting more and more people.' Naturally I agreed with them, but I only hope they will continue to be friends after reading what I have written.

For in researching into the origins of stress it has been necessary to dig deeply into the morass of life that we are all wallowing in, to examine the hypocrisy in our human relationships, and how we are rearing children to be prone to stress and unhappiness. And I haven't concentrated upon those unfortunate people who have to have a daily diet of tranquillizers, and the much maligned hypochondriacs, but looked at people, like my friends, who think they are normal and therefore immune.

In the pages that follow the reader may find certain of my conclusions unacceptable, or even incredible, but where possible I have tried to show how I arrived at them, and in any case the book has not been written so that I can set myself up as an oracle with all the answers to all the questions. Its object is to lift up a corner of the blanket of silence which has been covering the subject of stress for far too long.

Finally the reader is asked to appreciate that I am not a doctor of medicine or a psychiatrist, but have lectured extensively on this and allied subjects both in Britain and the United States of America, and the experience I have is the result of being a practising hypno-therapist and hypno-analyst for a number of years. I mention this because in certain chapters I may appear to be critical of the medical profession, therefore I must, in fairness to them, emphasize that the theme I have followed is not an attack on anyone, but an assessment of the society we have created, and are perpetuating.

Peter Blythe, 4 Stanley Place, Chester
30 September 1972

Chapter 1
Stress disease

'The pace of life in a modern society has speeded up to such a degree that we must expect to find an increasing number of people who are unable to cope with it.' That is how the subject of stress disease is blithely dismissed whenever it arises in the course of conversation. Unfortunately the facts are far more serious.

Authoritative medical opinion in the United States and Britain has gone on record to the effect that up to 70 per cent of all patients currently being treated by doctors in general practice are suffering from conditions which have their origins in unrelieved stress.

It is also recognized that certain stress diseases are lethal, and can kill just as successfully as a well-aimed bullet, and evidence to support this assertion can be found in the Thirteenth Report, No. 275, of the World Health Organization.

In the 1964 WHO Report the Committee on Mental Health listed those illnesses which are generally acknowledged to be psychosomatic – physical manifestations of mental stress – and among the ailments were the well known killers, coronary heart disease, diabetes mellitus and bronchial asthma.

Yet despite this knowledge the majority of doctors and the mass of the general public have adopted what can only be called the 'ostrich syndrome', where it is preferable to bury the head in the sand of everyday life and pretend the situation does not exist.

This attitude was strikingly illustrated by a psychiatrist who recently told a patient who had been referred to him, 'There is nothing wrong with you. You are just neurotic.'

What he failed to appreciate was that his female patient was already aware of his 'diagnosis', but as she was suffering from stress to the point where she was unable to eat or drink in the presence of strangers she wanted *help*. Admittedly the stress-factor was not of sufficient intensity to incapacitate her severely, although she did find it most distressing, and it prevented her from living a normal life.

Nor was her experience an isolated one. There is not a day which passes without many people going to see their doctor with varied complaints, only to be told, after a thorough examination, 'There is nothing wrong with you. It is all in your mind.' And this type of non-clinical assessment does not help the patient; instead it tends to aggravate the symptomatology because the statement implies either there is something wrong with them mentally, and that causes more anxiety, or the doctor is unable to ascertain the true cause of their problem and therefore it must be of a serious nature.

To be fair to the medical profession it has to be stated that current medical training does not include an in-depth study of psychodynamics (how the mind works and individually interprets the varied stimuli in a person's life style and their social environment), nor is psychosomatic medicine (how the mind can bring about physical malfunctioning) a part of the syllabus. However, in Britain there are now signs that attempts are being made to rectify these glaring omissions in the medical curriculum.

In 1971 a leading London psychiatrist addressed the Newcastle-upon-Tyne branch of the Royal College of General Practitioners on the subject of 'Whole Body Medicine'. He told the assembled doctors that the time had come when they should recognize that the patient who presented them with symptoms which could not be attributed to any ascertainable causes should not be dismissed as a neurotic and given a prescription for tranquillizers or anti-depressants. Instead he suggested that the doctors try to find out by asking whether anything had happened to the patient in his home life or at work which was causing the anxiety, and the need to be ill.

His talk had a mixed reception, and that was only to be expected for more than two thousand years ago the Greek philosopher Plato was advocating a 'whole body medicine' approach when he wrote, 'The cure of the part should not be attempted without treatment of the whole, and also no attempt should be made to cure the body without the soul, and therefore if the head and body are to be well, you must begin by curing the mind: that is the first thing . . . For this,' Plato continued, 'is the great error of our day in the treatment of the human body, that physicians separate the soul from the body.' And centuries later Dr Caleb Parry (1755–1822) wrote, 'It is much more important to know what sort of patient has a disease than what sort of disease he has.'

Further complicating the acceptance of the magnitude of stress diseases is the generally held jaundiced attitude which equates the stress-sufferer with the typical cartoon hypochondriac: the man who surrounds himself with a collection of different patent medicines and a vast assortment of pills, all meant to cure the plague of imaginary ills which constantly change from day to day.

The outcome of this prejudiced and inaccurate viewpoint is expressed in statements like, 'He just couldn't cope,' or 'If he pulled himself together he would be all right, because there is nothing wrong with him.' Both of these are derogatory, and they imply that the person who suffers what is colloquially known as a 'nervous breakdown' is an object to be pitied.

In our Western society this type of derision is reserved for members of the male sex, because women are still regarded as the 'weaker sex' and therefore much more likely to lose control and give way to attacks of hysteria.

And male chauvinism should not be made to shoulder all the blame for seeing every woman as a potential hysteric, as the history of medicine and the doctors of yesteryear provided a firm basis for this popular myth.

The word 'hysteria' is derived from the Greek word *hystera* meaning womb, and it was not too long ago that doctors thought that the woman who manifested a hysterical paralysis of a limb – when there was no organic reason for the symptom – was the victim of a moving womb. In a mysterious manner the womb had travelled into the affected area causing a blockage which, in turn, prevented normal functioning. Of course when surgery was performed to locate and remove the wandering womb there was no sign of it, but its absence did not cause the theory to be abandoned or revised. The fact that the womb was not where the surgeons expected to find it was neatly explained away by, 'It is understandable. Once surgery commenced it returned to its rightful place in the lower abdomen.'

Such an explanation now sounds incredible, nevertheless the theory is the source of the concept that we, the wombless men, could never suffer from hysteria, and if a man exhibited any hysterical symptoms they were a definite sign of a lack of manhood, and proof of weakness. To some extent the parents of today continue to indoctrinate their male children with the same outdated and dangerous attitude. A commonplace example will clarify the point being made. Let us imagine a six-year-old boy who is playing with some of his friends in the garden and falls down, hurting himself. He rushes into the house crying, wanting comfort, only to be told by one of his parents, 'Johnny, don't cry. You are a big boy now, and you know that big boys don't cry.'

If the imaginary Johnny had a twin sister and the same sort of accident happened to her, the outburst of tears would be dealt with differently. It would also be acceptable for her to occasionally give way to an emotional outburst and so obtain release from all the pent-up tension and frustration inside her, but let little Johnny try to use the identical emotional outlet and that would be anything but acceptable.

As a result of this conditioning, when the children grow up they continue to accept that women can cry without being considered weak or lacking in moral fibre; that a woman can let her hair down and show how upset she is. But not a man. He must be a *man* at all times. If he gets upset he must bottle up his feelings and never show them. He must go out and dig in the garden, chop wood, go for a long, brisk walk or indulge in other *manly* pursuits which, according to twentieth-century mythology, allow all the pent-up energy to be dissipated. The tragedy is that these activities rarely succeed in releasing the tension because they are not spontaneous and related to the specific cause. At best they will lower the tension a fraction, but the larger proportion will remain encased in the body, building up until it reaches a flashpoint, and the man explodes into a spasm of uncontrolled behaviour.

This facet of child-rearing also explains why many mild men

become aggressive after they have had a few drinks. The alcohol they imbibe weakens their ability to control their emotions, and the reservoir of residual tension bursts out. More important still it could be the reason why the male organism deteriorates more quickly than the female counterpart, and men die at an earlier age.

At this juncture these conclusions might appear to be too speculative, but in subsequent chapters my reasoning will, I hope, be borne out by additional evidence. However, before leaving the role of the *manly* man and its consequences, it is pertinent to note this is predominantly a trait confined to Northern Europe, North America and those former colonial nations whose white populations are of Anglo-Saxon origin. In Italy, the Mediterranean countries, Africa, etc., a man is allowed to express his feelings without being considered effeminate. But place these emotionally free men in a restrictive society and they too begin to succumb to stress disease.

One authentic account of this development was provided by Sir Heneage Ogilvie who, as editor of the British medical journal *The Practitioner*, wrote an introduction to Dr Hans Selye's book *The Stress of Life*,[1] and related his own observations during the Second World War when he was the surgeon in charge of some 200,000 Italian prisoners of war in Abyssinia.

The Italian doctors working in the camp hospitals had never, in their native country, seen cases of thrombo-angitis, also known as Burger's disease, where the blood vessels in the hands and feet become inflamed preventing free circulation, as a result of which these areas of the body ultimately become ulcerative and gangrenous. Consequently they were surprised to find it developing among the POWs. Sir Heneage Ogilvie attributed this phenomenon to the prisoners being confined and the resultant stress, and he commented how he had found the same clinical condition among men in Britain who worked under constant strain in the world of commerce.

But nothing I have mentioned so far defines exactly what a stress disease is, and how it evolves. An initial insight into an accurate formulation is found in the word 'disease', because if it

[1] Hans Selye, MD, *The Stress of Life*, Longmans, Green & Co. Ltd., London, 1957.

is broken down into its real meaning rather than accepting the face value of common usage it becomes apparent it refers to someone who is not at ease, i.e. they are 'dis-eased' by symptoms which prevent them from being relaxed and enjoying good health.

The next step is to recognize that the dis-eased patient's symptoms may be psychological or physical. And this is where the complexity arises, because there cannot be any psychological disturbance without a concomitant organic reaction, and neither can there be any organic malfunctioning that has not got psychological overtones.

To unravel this problem, a look at the effects of anxiety reveals the dynamic relationship which exists between the mind and body. Basically the state of anxiety is normal when the safety of the individual is threatened. Then the body prepares to fight off the threat or to run as fast as possible in flight from it.

When the brain (the mind) perceives the danger signal the autonomic nervous system, which is outside the control of consciousness, prepares for action by increasing the muscle tone – tensing up the muscles – and this leads to shallow breathing as the lungs are constricted. Sometimes this is accompanied by tremors or physical shaking if the response to the threat is delayed too long. There is also an increase of the heart rate, and its excessive pounding is felt as palpitations. The hands and feet perspire and in severe cases of fright the body disgorges surplus weight by emptying the bladder and bowels spontaneously. And if the threat appears to be insurmountable, the body can be overwhelmed by the musculature becoming rigid and then the person is really 'scared stiff'.

What I have just described is anxiety stemming from a real, objective threat to personal survival. But there is an identical physical reaction when the individual feels endangered by loss of prestige, security and love, and as everyone regularly finds themselves in situations where this can occur each member of the human race has developed what the late Professor Sigmund Freud and his daughter, Anna, have called 'ego defence mechanisms'.

There are many defence mechanisms that we all use daily

to cope with our feelings of dis-ease, yet for the purpose of studying the emergence of stress diseases it is sufficient to look at two of the most important: the Isolation of Effect and Repression.

When anything unpleasant happens it is a natural, human characteristic to try and stop ourselves from feeling our inner disquiet, sorrow, humiliation or whatever else is involved in a particular incident. To do this we prevent ourselves from recognizing our feelings or giving vent to them. We are prepared to remember every detail of what happened at a conscious, intellectual level, but we bury deep within us, in our unconscious mind and in the physical body, all the unpleasant feelings related to the event as they would be unbearable to us. The feelings still linger within us, unexpressed, and therefore we have *isolated the effects* from our consciousness. And the reason why this defence mechanism can have serious consequences is that, until all the pent-up feelings are recalled and released we may continue to feel 'dis-ease' without knowing why.

Should any incident be too horrific or too painful even to be remembered we repress *all traces of it from our recallable memory*, and it is just as if it had never happened. But it did, even though we dare not face it consciously, and those powerful repressed memories and feelings have to search for a more acceptable avenue of release.

All this may appear to be complicated, and this is because we humans are complicated animals. But certain examples will effectively illustrate how these two defence mechanisms can work to the detriment of well-being and continued ease. In two of the cases I have elected to quote, the reader will have the opportunity of seeing how anxiety activates a physical condition.

A young lady came to see me who was an agoraphobic (afraid of open spaces), and her condition had reached the point where she was unable to take her children to school or even go shopping at the local stores unless her husband accompanied her. During our initial sessions she could not even hazard a guess as to why she was frightened of going out of the house by herself. All she knew was that once she went through the front door of her home she had feelings of extreme panic, and was sure something terrible was going to happen to her. By using hypno-analysis we were able to bring back into her conscious mind a totally re-pressed memory of something which had occurred years before.

Her husband and she were Roman Catholics and did not use any type of birth control. They both tried to be careful, but when she discovered she was pregnant shortly after the birth of one of her children that was too much for her. She felt unable to accept the responsibility of a further child, so in desperation she tried to terminate her pregnancy by a folk-lore method which has little or no real abortive value. It was unsuccessful, but she had a mis-carriage weeks later.

The loss of her unborn child filled her with guilt. She felt it was God's way of punishing her for the 'sin' she had committed. From the moment she thought she was the object of her Maker's wrath she repressed all memory of the attempted abortion from consciousness. She remembered the loss of her unborn baby, but that was all.

It could be said that the defence mechanism protected her from dwelling upon her transgression, yet she was an agora-phobic.

When the repressed memory, and all its associated emotions were recalled and examined at a conscious level, the client dis-covered for herself why she could not leave the house. She was frightened that God would seize upon the opportunity to punish her further.

In the case of a second woman, she had been hospitalized as a catatonic schizophrenic, which meant that for a time she had been completely immobile, unable to move or speak, showed no reactions irrespective of what was done to her, or had had any contact with another human being.

As we talked together later she told me how she had an intense fear of men, and if a man came too near to her she became panic stricken. 'This fear became so strong that it made me ill, and I had my attack.' Slowly she began to see that her defence mechan-ism served two purposes.

While she was catatonic and devoid of all feeling she was safe from any male advances made towards her, allowing her to escape from the inner turmoil of tension. At the same time her immobility was also a safeguard.

She had a violent urge to take revenge upon men for what they were doing to her. That placed her in a further dilemma, for to carry out her urges was contrary to everything she had been taught by her parents. Her mind, battered by the conflict, solved it by making her incapable of taking any action, by bringing on the catatonic seizure.

This example of catatonia illustrates another Freudian concept as to how people unconsciously produce paralysis, blindness, lameness and other physical manifestations as a means of coping with anxiety.

Andrew, a young man with an anxiety state and a deep distrust of all women, showed how there is a simple logic behind many of the symptoms presented to a psychotherapist. During his analysis it was ascertained that something happened to him when he was nine years of age which had a direct bearing upon his present condition.

He knew, and was able to talk about, how he was sent away to his first boarding school. His mother had been forced into sending him away to school because his father had left home and it was necessary for her to make a career to support both of them financially.

Andrew was then hypnotized, regressed back to his first few days at the school when he was nine years old, and he re-experienced all the horror and fear he had felt then. He told his therapist that nobody loved him. His father did not love him, because he had left home, and now he was sure his mother did not love him either otherwise she would not have sent him away.

His entire body was writhing as the emotions he had isolated over the years from his recallable memory returned, and he became frightened of the effect they were having upon his body. At that point the therapist terminated the hypnotic state, and as he did so Andrew cried out in panic, 'I can't move my right arm. What is wrong with me?'

Despite all his attempts to move his arm it remained paralysed. The therapist knew the psychosomatic paralysis was a defence mechanism, and asked, 'If you could move your right arm, what would you do?'

Andrew remained silent, more concerned about trying to restore movement to the arm.

'Come on, tell me, tell me, what would you do if you could move your right arm at this moment?' the therapist demanded.

The answer was immediate.

'I would kill the fucking bitch,' Andrew shouted as he lashed out viciously with his right arm.

After the outburst had subsided the therapist and his patient talked about what had happened, and Andrew was able to see why he needed to paralyse his arm to prevent him from leaving the office, going home and possibly committing an act of violence on his mother which his conscious mind knew would be wrong.

What has been discussed on the preceding pages has been part of the Freudian theory of anxiety and tension, and while it makes a considerable contribution to an understanding of stress diseases there are other theories which are equally pertinent and have to be mentioned.

Three American doctors, Gerhard B. Haugen, MD, Henry H. Dixon, MD, and Herman A. Dickel, MD, see the anxiety state as a learned physical reaction. The publisher's introduction to their book *A Therapy for Anxiety Tension Reactions*[2] states:

The anxious patient, the authors observe, has since childhood braced himself as if to meet danger. When he reaches adulthood tensing and bracing are to him as automatic as breathing. This state of chronic tension causes, directly, all the patient's somatic symptoms, and indirectly, all of his psychic symptoms. The authors found that training the chronically 'nervous' patient to relax (using a modified Jacobson System) brings relief to both the psychic and somatic symptoms . . .

Briefly what Drs Haugen, Dixon and Dickel postulate is that during childhood and adolescence the patient finds himself anxious due to external or internal threats to his well-being, and the body tenses up. Then, when the moment of threat has passed the body relaxes, but not completely, and there remains inside the body a small amount of residual tension. The next time the patient knows arousal there is again muscular tension, yet when

[2] The Macmillan Company, New York, 1963.

it passes a larger residue of physical tension remains. Before long, as a result of the incomplete discharge of tension, the body finds itself permanently tensed up, although there is no threat to account for the physical state of arousal.

With the body unable to relax certain symptoms begin to appear. They may be digestive disorders, an exaggerated heart beat, insomnia, continual headaches, or other indications of anxiety which have their origins in the mind, but have become rooted in the body, i.e. somatized. Others react psychologically. The brain/mind receives the messages from the body telling it that the body is ready to fight or flee from a threat, and yet the brain/mind cannot locate anything tangible to account for the physical preparedness. Such an anomaly cannot be tolerated for long, and to bring about the unified working of the body and mind the brain/mind has to invent something to be frightened of, like a fear of heights, open spaces, dirt, germs, etc.

This hypothesis has gained wide credence for it is now standard practice for patients suffering from psychological and somatized anxiety states to attend relaxation classes as out-patients at their local mental hospital.

Outside the medical sphere thousands claim they have obtained relief from attending Yoga classes and learning the Eastern method of relaxation, and it may explain why those practitioners using hypnosis have a large percentage of success, as the hypnotic session teaches the client to relax both mentally and physically.

However, before everyone rushes out to the nearest relaxation class I believe that relaxation alone will not bring about a remission of symptoms for everyone. If the patient's symptomatology is due to a repressed event, or an isolation of effect; if the disease is due to a lack of attention, then individual psychotherapy remains the only reliable method of treatment.

Another theory which is compatible with both the Freudian and Haugen, Dixon and Dickel findings, is the earlier work of the controversial psychiatrist, Dr Wilhelm Reich, who died on 3 November 1957 and is regarded by many as one of the founders of modern psychosomatic medicine.

Reich believed the body contained a Life Force, and this needs to flow freely inside the body if it is to remain healthy. The problems arise and disease creeps in, according to Reich, when the energy becomes anchored in one part of the body, or the overall physical structure becomes inflexible.

In his book *Character Analysis*[3], Reich showed how the body mirrors the general tensions and general character of the patient, and states that before an analyst can assist a patient to become fully functioning, the body defences, which prevent the free flow of energy, have initially to be broken down.

A further illustration might be useful here. To avoid feeling the unpleasant responses that come into effect when faced with an alarm situation, a man may learn to tighten his stomach muscles. The first time he does this, the muscles relax again once the situation has passed. Yet when he meets a similar situation he has already learned how to counteract the physical unpleasantness, and the stomach muscles tighten automatically. If this process is repeated too often and at frequent intervals there quickly comes a time when the muscles are held permanently rigid. This character armouring, for this is what it becomes, no longer serves as an adjustment to tension, rather it prevents the flow of a healthy Life Force, and is a mal-adjustment.

What is even more interesting is that during therapy sessions Reich found that when he relaxed a patient's muscular armouring the latter would recall the original event which made it necessary. His discovery has been confirmed by many other prominent practitioners.

While I was in New York City researching this book I met and talked with Dr Alexander Lowen, a famous American psychiatrist and neo-Reichian, at his Institute for Bioenergetic Analysis on Park Avenue, and he told me his Bioenergetic Therapy is based upon Reich's work.

Over here in the United Kingdom in the summer of 1971 I talked with a prominent British psychotherapist, Glynn Seaborne-Jones, PhD, and he said that on many occasions he was able to release repressed and traumatic memories by applying pressure to certain rigid parts of the body.

He explained to me that his primary task was to get the patient to move freely and once that had been accomplished the ar-

[3] The Noonday Press, New York, 1967 edition.

moured area would present itself to him. Then he would proceed to work on that one spot, and even if the patient did recall a repressed memory it did not mean that a 'cure' was immediately effected. 'It is more like a draining process,' he said, and at subsequent sessions he had to ascertain if there was 'still some pus in the boil'.

He meant that if the patient still retained some of the character armour when they next met he would return to working on the same part of the body, possibly eliciting further incidents which were, in some way, related to the initial one.

Of course Seaborne-Jones knew of Reich's work, but an Israeli practitioner of acupuncture, Giora Harel, who had no knowledge of Reich, found the same thing happening when he used deep massage to relax some of his patients.

Trygve Braaty noticed that some of his patients receiving physiotherapy would be engulfed by painful memories when their arm muscles were being relaxed.[4]

There are only two more major theorists to be examined before we can return and find an accurate and acceptable definition of what I mean when I refer to a stress disease. The first of these is Alfred Adler, who like Reich broke away from Freud's early circle to expound the concept that people are continually seeking to overcome their feelings of inferiority, which cause anxiety, by striving to gain power over others. And one of the ways of obtaining this is by retreating into illness.

'You cannot get married immediately, and leave me. You know that my heart isn't strong enough for me to live alone.' That is the universally recognized appeal of a domineering mother who does not want her daughter to grow up and be independent, and if the daughter persists in her intention of leaving home the mother can and does produce all the symptoms of a classic coronary thrombosis. All too often this blackmail by illness is successful, and when domination is firmly re-established the mother is free from any further symptoms until her authority is about to be flouted again.

What these domineering mothers do not appreciate is that they are employing a dangerous strategy, because if it is used fre-

[4] *Fundamentals of Psychoanalytic Technique*, Wiley, New York, 1954.

quently the mind has the habit of producing the real physical illness, and that is often fatal.

Although this imaginary mother/daughter power struggle is not very subtle, and some of the manoeuvres used both consciously and unconsciously in the retreat into illness can be complicated, it highlights the Adlerian hypothesis that there can be a logical cause for disease other than infections.

And this brings us to Dr Georg Groddeck (1866–1934) a German physician who had his practice in the spa town of Baden-Baden, and who can rightly be called the father of psychosomatic medicine even though the term was used at the beginning of the nineteenth century.

Quite independently of Sigmund Freud, Groddeck came to the conclusion that behind every manifestation of illness there was a reason, and the afflicted organ or limb was specifically selected by a part of the mind which he called 'the It' (das Es), and if 'the It's' motives could be analysed and understood then the patient would recover.

In Groddeckian analysis the way in which we describe our ailments provides many clues.

'I have caught a cold,' really means in Groddeckian terms, 'I needed to catch a cold at this moment in time to fulfil a personal need.'

'I have broken my leg,' is accepted as meaning, 'I have been in an accident, and the outcome of it was that my leg was broken.' But not to Groddeck. He would ask, 'Why did you need to break your leg?' and would expect, and get, an answer which would give him an insight into why the patient needed to place himself in a position where an accident could occur.

When a sore throat prevented speech, Groddeck would want to know, 'Why do you need to be unable to speak?'

If a patient contracted an infection, the question likely to be put to him was, 'Why have you infected yourself? What is it that drove you to cause some of the germs around you and within you to multiply so that you were able to use them to make yourself ill?'[5]

He also used the same type of organ analysis with many

[5] Georg Groddeck, The Unknown Self, Vision Press, London, 1967.

patients who went to his clinic suffering from heart disease, chronic kidney infection (nephritis), eye conditions and cancer. In fact he applied it to everyone, and the results he obtained were remarkable as the case of the English translator of his books, Miss M. V. E. Collins, reveals.

Miss Collins went to meet Groddeck in 1925 after several specialists had diagnosed that she was suffering from syringo-melia, a rare and slowly deteriorating disease affecting the spinal cord, and had agreed that within five years she would be confined to her home. After receiving treatment in Baden-Baden she began to learn German, and died in 1956, some twenty-five years after the expiration of the time allotted when she should have been bed-ridden.[6]

Another of his often quoted successes was an unnamed woman he started to treat in 1921 with general oedema (dropsy) due to a combined heart and kidney malfunctioning. At the end of the fourth week of treatment Groddeck got his patient to talk about the problem which was preventing her making a speedy recovery.

Basically it was that when she was a young girl she had wanted, desperately, to become a nun, but her parents did not approve, and while she accepted their decision she solemnly swore to God that she would remain virginal throughout her life. Later she married, and from then onwards she had been perpetually troubled by her conscience. In the confessional she had told her priest about the oath she had broken, and he assured her that the promise she had made in her youth was not binding, therefore her guilt was unnecessary. 'Still I never lose my burden of anxiety nor find any peace of mind,' she said.

After she had revealed her guilty secret to Groddeck, and he left the room she began to urinate copiously. Four hours later she had lost 11 lbs in weight, and a further 2 lbs 3 ounces by morning. A week later she had lost a total of 46 lbs 3 ounces (25 kilos), and was able to return home free from her earlier symptom.[7]

Groddeck's views and his analysing of organic conditions may well sound like witchcraft, but in the years I have been in practice

[6] Carl M. Grossman, MD, and Sylva Grossman, *The Wild Analyst: The Life and Work of Georg Groddeck*, Barrie and Rockliff, London, 1965.
[7] See Georg Groddeck, *The Unknown Self*, Vision Press, London, 1967.

as a lay-psychotherapist I have seen confirmation of his claims.

On many occasions I have asked people with severe headaches, 'All right, you have got a headache, but why do you need it? What is there you do not want to recognize or think about?' And after a period of time, when they deny any knowledge of the precipitating factors, they have recognized why they needed it and after discussing the worrisome topic the headache has disappeared.

I remember a lady who complained about her stiff neck, and although it was not the reason why she came to see me it was annoying her. She said it was the result of washing her hair four days before, then sitting in a draught afterwards. It was a perfectly logical explanation, but as we had got to know each other well in the course of therapy I wondered if it fulfilled an unconscious need.

'Is there any reason why you have felt, over the past few days, a need to keep a level head on your shoulders?'

She began to laugh. 'I know what you are getting at,' she replied. 'You think my stiff neck is psychosomatic, don't you?'

I could not deny it, and repeated the same question in another way. 'Have you felt over the last few days that you could, quite easily, do something you would be sorry for later, and consequently have had to keep a level head on your shoulders?' That time she thought about what I had asked her.

'I'm sure this has nothing to do with my stiff neck, that is purely physical, but last Friday I went round to see two friends of mine, a man and his wife. They are both very pleasant, but recently I have had the idea that the husband would like to make love to me.

'There was nothing tangible. It was the way he looked at me, and the little things that he did which made me think he was putting pressure on me. He is a nice man,' she continued, 'and while I am not physically attracted to him, I had the feeling, if he maintained the pressure, I might find myself letting him. It is all too silly really, feeling I might agree, because I didn't – no, I don't – want him to make love to me. Yet, because it was on my mind I decided, before I went round to see them on the Friday night, I would be on my guard, and remain a little aloof.'

'And when did you get your stiff neck?' I enquired.

'I woke up with it on Friday morning,' she answered.

We then talked about the situation and her feelings, during which she agreed she had no need to 'keep her head firmly on her shoulders', as she was not going to have sexual intercourse with him under any circumstances.

'How is your neck now?' I asked.

She moved it gently, and then more quickly from side to side. 'Isn't that amazing, it has gone.'

Another lady was coming to see me for our weekly meeting, when she arrived she had some unpleasant mouth ulcers which made speech difficult. In answer to my question, she told me they had appeared at work, and it transpired that, inadvertently, she had said something to a friend which was the truth, but unkind. 'I didn't mean it to hurt her. I just said what I thought without thinking about the effect it would have on her. I could have bitten my tongue off the moment I had said it.'

As she still felt guilty I suggested that as soon as she arrived at work the following morning she could explain to her friend what she had really meant, and apologize for her thoughtlessness.

The next morning her mouth was still inflamed, but within fifteen minutes of speaking to her friend the discomfort had disappeared, her ulcerated gums lost their angry look, and the accompanying burning sensation had gone.

Whereas my own experiences are supportive of Groddeck's theory they are unacceptable as scientific proof. For evidence backed up by exhaustive research it is necessary to look elsewhere mainly to the work of Dr Harold G. Wolff, an American neurologist at Cornell University, New York, and a group of his colleagues who began to investigate causation factors in illness in the latter part of the 1930s.

The doctors involved in the experiments got more than 5,000 patients to tell them about changes in their life-styles which had occurred prior to the onset of their particular symptoms, and made a note of them. Attention was paid to those suffering from colds and nasal infections. These patients were asked to return when they had recovered.

Upon their return tests were carried out to ensure they were free from their nasal complaints, and then the conversation was concentrated upon discussing the changes in the life-style which had taken place before they 'caught' their colds. Further nasal tests were made when the talk was terminated, and it was found that getting the patient to talk about the earlier life-style changes brought about the re-activation of the cold symptoms.

The significance of this work has been ignored by medical research, and this is a pity, because Wolff may have discovered why there is no cure for the common cold; that those who catch it have a need to cause the available germs to multiply within themselves.

However, to continue a review of the evidence, not long ago British television screened a programme about the work undertaken by Dr Richard H. Rahe and men of the US Navy. Rahe looked at the changes in the life-style of 2,500 officers and men in the six months preceding his study, and then kept a close check upon the health of his guinea-pigs during the following six months they spent at sea.

Those who scored highly on the 'Social Readjustment Rating Scale' as a result of life-style changes were found to have 90 per cent more illnesses than those who had a low score.

The outcome of this research, according to the television programme was that the US Navy Department was able to screen sailors due to go on long, submerged voyages aboard nuclear-powered submarines, and those who fell into the high-risk category were prevented from joining the crew.

In November 1971, the British Sunday newspaper *The Observer*[8] printed an item under the heading, 'Why a change is not always as good as a rest,' giving the conclusions of work done by Dr Thomas H. Holmes, Professor of Psychiatry at Washington University.

Dr Holmes and his team set out to establish the feasibility of predicting the onset of illness so that preventive action could be taken. People in many countries were tested. In America, Japan, Spain, France, Switzerland, Sweden and Denmark, the examination of men and women from all social classes showed similar results; that major upheavals and changes in the pattern of living,

[8] Issue dated 7 November 1971.

whether pleasant or unpleasant, bring about stress, and if cumulative effects go beyond a certain stress-level physical illness develops.

The Observer informed its readers that Dr Holmes had been involved in research into the effects of stress for twenty years, and 'during his early researches Dr Holmes found that the onset of certain illnesses – among them tuberculosis, skin diseases, some cancers and heart disease – correlated closely with major changes in life style, such as moving house, divorce, or death of a close relative.'

Under the title 'Psychosomatic Syndrome', with the subtitle, 'When mother-in-law or other disaster's visit, a person can develop a bad, bad cold. Or worse', the same Dr Thomas H. Holmes, together with Minoru Masuda, gave further details of their work in the April 1972 issue of the widely read and authoritative American monthly magazine *Psychology Today*.[9]

While discussing the correlation between life-style changes and emergent illness, they emphasized that the preceding events did not have to be traumatic, such as the death of a marriage partner, or being sentenced to a term of imprisonment, but were an accumulation of what could be considered as everyday tension producing episodes, such as a child leaving home, changing a job, or a deep family disagreement.

When they got a number of doctors to qualify the seriousness of 125 diseases they found there was 'a highly significant correlation between life-change scores and chronic disease (leukemia, cancer, heart attack, schizophrenia, menstrual difficulties and warts)'.

Another observation was that women, both married and single, were more likely to conceive at those times when there were striking changes in their way of life. This is of personal interest, because when I was writing a paper on various aspects of conception, back in 1963–4, a psychiatrist and myself were trying to provide an explanation as to why women who were victims of criminal rape conceived more readily than women having regular sexual intercourse. Holmes and Masuda have now provided the answer through their research. But without wishing to detract

9 *Psychology Today*, 1330 Camino del Mar, Del Mar, California 92014.

from their findings in any way, this has been recognized, if only instinctively, by women over the centuries, and is expressed in the old English adage, 'A new house, a new baby'.

Nor is the concept that the loss of livelihood, an abortive love affair, or the death of a dearly loved and close relative, can be the genesis of disease, for according to the late Dr J. A. C. Brown this was accepted as a fact by medical practitioners until the early part of the nineteenth century.[10]

Even Georg Groddeck's idea that accidents are also expressions of an inner desire to injure oneself have been confirmed by subsequent research.

Back in 1934 Dr Flanders Dunbar of the Presbyterian Hospital in New York found while she was studying the underlying psychological factors in organic disease, 80 per cent of the people in her control group who had suffered from fractures due to an 'accident' were unconsciously motivated towards self-injury and a more recent study made by Steve Bramwell of American footballers who had suffered injury on the football field showed that seven out of the ten college men with multiple injuries had high scores when changes in their life-styles were computed, while at the other end of the scale, only 10 per cent of those with a low score were injured in the course of the football season.[11]

After this lengthy diversion the question still has to be answered, 'How does a stress disease evolve?'

Earlier in this chapter I showed that anxiety activates a physical response through the autonomic nervous system, and that, in turn, creates a state of body tension.

The dictionary I have on my desk defines 'tension' as 'stretching; a pulling strain; stretched or strained state; strain generally', and it is not necessary to be an engineer, either mechanical or human, to know that when anything, a piece of metal, elastic, or the human body, is subjected to continual tension or stretching strain this must result in a breakdown of the part submitted to the strain.

A descriptive comparison is metal fatigue in an aircraft. As a plane is expensive it is kept in the air, flying passengers and earn-

[10] J. A. C. Brown, *Freud and the Post-Freudians*, Penguin, 1967 edition.
[11] See *Psychology Today*, April 1972.

ing money continually, except for the times it is grounded for maintenance. By flying through wind, rain and simply because of the speed it flies at, the metal structure of the body is kept under stress. That weakens the metal and it suffers from fatigue, and if the weakened part is not detected by the mechanics during routine maintenance – and it usually is, because the airline companies believe in preventive medicine – it collapses under the strain of flight, with the resultant loss of passenger life. Exactly the same thing happens with the human body!

Now we can see that stress disease evolves when a part of the body is submitted to unrelieved anxiety, kept in a state of constant tension, placing undue stress upon it, until the part collapses and ceases to function.

Chapter 2
Symptoms of the plague

The actual extent of the plague is difficult to ascertain owing to the lack of available figures which incorporate all the varied stress diseases, therefore one is dependent upon governmental reports issued periodically, data provided by responsible medical practitioners, and statements appearing in both the professional and popular press. However, accepting these limitations, if this line of investigation is pursued a fragment of the overall picture does emerge.

During a conversation in 1971 an executive of a British pharmaceutical company told me that virtually half the drugs being prescribed by doctors fell under the blanket-heading of 'psychiatric drugs', which includes tranquillizers, anti-depressants, sleeping pills, etc.

His assertion has not been officially corroborated as far as I know, but an official report stated that in England and Wales in 1969 doctors wrote out fifteen million prescriptions for tranquillizers and five million for anti-depressants.

A further report issued by the Royal College of General Practitioners revealed that the use of psychotropic drugs, the minor tranquillizers and hypnotics, had increased by 20 per cent in the five years from 1965 to 1970, and amounted to nearly fifty million prescriptions annually. The author of the report, Dr Peter Parish of Bristol, posed the question. 'The increase in the prescribing of CNS depressant drugs suggests that general practitioners are blanketing their patients' emotional reactions to an excessive degree and they must ask themselves whether it is right for them to produce a pharmacological leucotomy on contemporary society.'[1]

[1] Dr Peter Parish, 'The Prescribing of Psychotropic Drugs in General Practice', *General Practitioner*, January 1972.

A medical spokesman interviewed on a radio programme, on 11 August 1972, said that 60 per cent of the British population were taking tranquillizers or sleeping pills.

And none of these statistics take into account the hundreds of millions of aspirin – three tons of which are swallowed daily in Britain alone – phenacetin, codeine, and other patent medicines which are freely purchased at the local store and chemist by those afflicted with stress headaches and stress stomach upsets.

This enormous aspirin consumption provides more than an indication as to the amount of stress in the country and an article in the weekly medical journal *General Practitioner*,[2] written by Dr Robin Murray MRCP, shows that this attempt to relieve stress symptoms can be dangerous and even fatal.

Dr Murray claims that more people die from 'abusing headache pills than heroin,' and out of 7,000 patients who are admitted to hospital yearly suffering from gastro-intestinal bleeding through taking aspirins, approximately 250 die.

Looking at another aspect of the plague, agoraphobia, there are approximately a quarter of a million agoraphobics in Britain who are confined to their homes, and Mr Grenville Janner, MP for Leicester North-West, said early in 1972, 'The numbers are vast, but little is done. The Government doesn't spend enough money, there is not enough research . . . We're just sweeping the problem under the carpet.' Mrs Alice Neville, a leading member of the agoraphobics' organization, 'Open Door', clarified the position further by commenting that included in the figure of a quarter of a million sufferers were 50,000 children of school age.[3]

Yet another report, this time referring to migraine and published by the Office of Health Economics in London, in June 1972, estimated that as many as five million people were afflicted by this type of excruciating headache.

Nor is the situation any better in other Western countries. Back in the 1960s Professor George Mouly of Miami University wrote that out of a hundred American children, randomly selected, four or five would be hospitalized in mental hospitals; another four or five would be seriously mentally ill but cared for

2 Issue dated 7 January 1972.
3 *News of the World*, 9 April 1972.

in special institutions other than mental hospitals; one or two would be convicted and imprisoned for criminal, anti-social acts; three or four would be so severely mentally retarded that they would not be in a position to live normal lives, and out of the remaining eighty-eight children between thirty and fifty would fall into the category 'deeply neurotic'.[4]

A further look at the United States of America reveals that its people swallow five thousand million pills a year to help them quieten their anxieties, to counter-act depression, to help them to sleep, and to pep them up. In fact this assumed such gigantic proportions that in 1971 Senator Edward Kennedy asked the Congress of the USA to write into the Congressional Record a paper sounding the alarm about the dangers of 'internal pollution'.

It would be easy for me to go on quoting report after report, but as they all carry the same message – that mankind is being stretched to breaking point – it is more relevant to look at the symptoms instead of writing down one set of statistics after another. For statistics are impersonal, and it is the prevailing impersonality reflected in all strata of our society that makes a major contribution to the problem of stress disease.

Before launching into what ailments have their roots in anxiety-tension-stress, the question I am repeatedly asked when lecturing on the subject is, 'Why is it that some people develop psychoneurotic conditions, and others manifest their stress through psychosomatic illnesses?'

With our limited knowledge no one can give a definite answer, but the hypothesis accepted by many psychotherapists is that the solution may be found in a child's relationship with its parents, especially the mother. If, in the formulative years, a child gains the desired attention by emotional outbursts, and is otherwise ignored, then as an adult he or she will have been conditioned into accepting that the only way to obtain loving care is to express their needs psychoneurotically. On the other hand, if the child is rejected when it reacts emotionally, and receives a positive response when it is ill, by the time he or she matures

[4]G. Mouly, *Psychology for Effective Teaching*, Holt, Rhinehart & Winston, Inc., New York, 1968.

illness will have become synonymous with love and attention.

This latter learning process often becomes apparent in a patient being treated for a psychosomatic condition. For as he is helped to understand the unconscious meaning behind the disability the physical symptoms disappear, to be replaced with a psychoneurotic one. These can alternate for a time with the patient trying to manoeuvre the therapist into abandoning objective assistance, and becoming emotionally involved – the equivalent of the earlier, longed for parental love. If the therapist falls into the trap, then the therapist and therapy cease to be of value because the patient has proved he can get attention by being ill, and the same 'I'm going to be ill' syndrome will be activated whenever the patient has the need to be comforted.

To try and prevent children from learning how to retreat into illness to obtain love the New York psychiatrist, Dr Murray Banks, used to urge parents in his lectures never to show more love to their sick child than they did normally. His advice is hard to follow and members of his audiences thought he was exaggerating its importance. He was not. Daily many adults, mostly married men who are employees, re-enact the sick child role.

They awaken one morning still feeling tired and lethargic, and the prospect of going to work where they are an unrecognized cipher in a large complex is anything but appealing. But to admit to their wives, 'Darling, I feel too tired and miserable to go to work today, so I think I will spend the day in bed,' is an admission which leaves them wide open to the criticism of being bone-idle, or the stinging retort, 'If I have to get up, get the kids off to school, and do the housework, you have got to get up and go to work. I am not going to slave away while you lie in bed expecting to be waited upon hand and foot. So, up you get, and be quick about it, or you will be late.'

Rather than face that, and be made to feel like a selfish child, it is easier for them to say, 'Darling, I don't feel too well today. Would you be a pet and telephone the office to say that I am sick?' as that approach calls for sympathy. 'Oh, you poor dear. Where do you feel ill? Do you want me to telephone the doctor? Would you like me to bring you up a cup of tea to bed?' is the response that takes them back to being the loved child again, and is tantamount to permission to indulge themselves. Sometimes these males put on such a good act to convince their wives that the illness becomes real as the day goes on, and they require a couple of days to recover. When that happens the original tiredness, an excuse to avoid unpleasantness, is converted into a real feeling of sickness. A simple example of psychosomatics at work!

In addition to childhood conditioning, the illness a person has can communicate the individual need and character. The sufferer from colitis (chronic diarrhoea) can be a sensitive person living in a restrictive atmosphere where he cannot give rein to his feelings, and as he cannot contain himself permanently he loses control of his bowels. In the same way any affected organ of the body can be the outward expression of an internal emotional conflict.

There are no hard and fast rules governing 'organ language', yet skin diseases can often be correctly interpreted as meaning that the patient has an unconscious dread he or she is unclean.

A young man in his early twenties sought my help after hearing I had had a measure of success in helping those with facial acne. He told me his facial eruptions were most disfiguring when he wanted to look his best, namely when he was going out on a date with a girl, and he was sure that it was the angry blemishes on his face which had prevented him from being at ease with women, and responsible for his not having found a regular girl friend.

It transpired he had many male friends with whom he spent most of his leisure moments, therefore he was not an isolate whose lack of confidence prevented him from making any relationships. The trouble lay in his dealings with the opposite sex.

I asked him for his opinion of young women in general. He saw the girls he could meet in the places where young people congregate as amateur prostitutes and a far cry from the mental image he carried of the ideal girl – demure, free from make-up, loyal and free from guile. In his comparison lay the crux of his conflict. Still a sexual virgin, he had been made to understand the sexual act outside marriage was taboo, and masturbation was neither acceptable nor necessary. He wanted to live up to those moral values, but he masturbated, and that sexual outlet made him feel unclean, causing his skin to reflect it in acne. When he made plans to take a girl out, the thing he most wanted was to seduce her. That being unacceptable his acne flared up because of his guilty desire for sexual intercourse, and it also served him well as a defence mechanism. The girls were deterred by his facial appearance so they did not go out with him a second time, and their decision protected him from the fear he might lose control.

A number of men and women may have the same complaint, they may share general aetiology, but each one will have a different, personal reason.

Following the trail of symptom and illness language, I will describe the case of a woman in her mid-thirties who sought treatment for her bladder. Whenever she left home she could not go for more than ten or fifteen minutes without having to urinate. This could have been diagnosed as an anxiety state – an exaggeration of the 'fight or flight' mechanism mentioned earlier – and a series of doctors made this error with the result that she thought she was incurable because the tranquillizers they prescribed for her had no effect.

Driven as a last resort into seeing a psychotherapist he discovered she was a very unhappy person, whose life, from her standpoint, was a succession of one sad day after another.

She could talk about how miserable her life was, but she admitted that irrespective of how much she wanted to, she could not release the inner sadness and cry. Oh yes, she wanted to cry. Her eyes were always red just as if she had been crying, but never more than a couple of tears oozed out to relieve her misery. The way her unconscious mind resolved her problem was to equate the water of her unshed tears with the water of urination. She couldn't cry through the tear ducts, so she cried through the urethra.

As we live in an age of mass-medicine the individuality of disease tends to be pushed aside. The medical profession wants charts naming the psychosomatic illnesses, and alongside them be provided with a brief summary of the personality types prone to the particular ailment. Thus they hope to say, 'He suffers from coronary thrombosis. That always applies to over-industrious people who are always tense and anxious to prove themselves by taking all the responsibility upon themselves.'

This is a dangerous pipe-dream. It does not answer questions like, 'Why does he need to prove himself?' 'Why cannot he relax?' 'What is causing his compulsion to over-work?' Only when the individual has given answers to these and other questions can he be helped to live and enjoy a fuller life.

Having made that point, now we can compile a list showing what ailments are recognized to have a stress background.

Hypertension – high blood pressure
Coronary thrombosis
Migraine
Hay fever, and allergies
Asthma
Pruritus – intense itching
Peptic ulcers
Constipation
Colitis
Rheumatoid arthritis
Menstrual difficulties
Nervous dyspepsia – flatulence and indigestion
Hyperthyroidism – over-active thyroid gland
Diabetes mellitus
Skin disorders
Tuberculosis

This list is made up from various responsible sources,[5] but does not tell us too much about those who suffer from them.

For instance, Dr Lester A. Millikin of St Louis, Missouri, worked for a number of years with arthritics, and he found by using hypno-analysis that the onset of the condition was always precipitated by an emotional upset which made his patients hold themselves rigid. Once they ventilated their repressed feelings he was able to restore a large degree of mobility.

Much of my own work has been with clients suffering from migraine, and while I could provide a generalized character analysis – they are people who have a need to be liked and loved, and when they are placed in untenable positions, not knowing

[5] The World Health Organization Report; issue no. 3 of *Acta Psychosomatica*, issued by the international pharmaceutical company, J. R. Geigy, plus conversations with experts in this field of medicine.

how to act, have an attack – the reason why they have that type of character has to be probed.

Nor is the above list, in my opinion, comprehensive enough, so let us journey into deeper and murkier waters.

When faced with stress-laden situations which cannot be resolved through circumstances or fear of the outcome, some people have a tendency to lose their appetite, and this is acknowledged to be normal. Yet when this is carried to extreme, usually by younger women, the appetite can disappear completely, becoming the clinical condition known as *anorexia nervosa*. If this happens the loss of weight is abnormal through starvation, and despite excellent medical care can end with death.

The few anorexia patients I have come into contact with, and I must admit they are few in number, all had a strong desire to be little girls and devoid of adult responsibility. In keeping with the little girl theory, which I put in here to promote thought and investigation and not as a fact, these women regress back to pre-puberty by a cessation of menstrual periods. Yes, I am aware this may well be the result of anaemia, due to starvation, but why the need to starve? And those I have met have yearned for physical demonstrations of love which women of their chronological ages cannot expect to obtain.

Having mentioned weight, this would appear to be a good time to discuss obesity. If we discount over-weight due to glandular disturbance, a foolish premise as the glandular (endocrine) system is affected by stress, there are three reasons for people being over-weight. Firstly, there are the habit-eaters: those who have learned to eat more than the body requires. At the end of a talk I gave on this subject a man said, 'I am not a compulsive eater, and I'm not eating any more than I have always done, but I am putting on weight. Apparently I don't fit into your theories, so can you explain why?'

As an adherent of the school of psychological thought which believes that for every human action there must be a reason, I countered his question with a question. 'You might not be eating any more than you did in the past, but has your life-style changed recently?'

He told me he had been a professional athlete, but as he had passed the peak of his performance he had retired. At that moment he started to smile. 'I see now what you are getting at. I am a habit-eater. I now have a sedentary occupation, but I am still eating as much as I did when I was an athlete. I don't need the same amount of food now, and my body, instead of converting it into the energy I needed in the old days, is converting it into fat.'

Secondly, we meet the compulsive eaters who have an uncontrollable urge to eat whenever they are unhappy, anxious or lonely, even though they are not hungry. The origins of this are found in the way children are reared in Western society. Possibly the only time a child is cuddled by the mother is when it is fed, and this establishes an association between food and love. This is often re-inforced by mothers using food to bribe their children, 'If you are a good boy I will give you some money for chocolate.' 'If you are a good girl you can have a second portion of ice-cream.' 'Now eat up all your dinner like a good boy,' and if the boy is not hungry and still refuses to eat up what is left on the plate his mother becomes angry with him. Therefore it is natural that some unhappy adults have a strong tendency to regress back to their childhood when they are under stress and attempt to re-capture the sense of security provided by the mother and food.

Another aspect of anxiety is an impression of emptiness in the stomach which is temporarily alleviated by the additional intake of food. But the extra food does not solve anything, it re-inforces the compulsion as it becomes a habit.

The third reason for obesity is the way it serves as a defence mechanism. Many over-weight women have an unconscious need to be fat and physically unattractive to protect them from anxiety-provoking sexual advances from men, even their husbands. This often makes itself known when they are dieting. As the pounds slip away, the stress then becomes unbearable, and the only answer for them is to forget all about losing weight and remain fat.

What I have written is recognized by various doctors. A psychiatrist told me that an obese woman we both knew 'wanted stuffing vaginally, and because she couldn't accept that, she is stuffing herself orally.' And Dr Eugene Scheimann of Chicago wrote an article for *Forum – The International Journal of Human Relations*[6] entitled 'Thin is beautiful ... but plump is sexier' in which he advocates a sex diet based upon, 'Don't reduce – seduce'. It is good advice even if it does ignore the existence of the fat girl's fear of sex, hence her fatness, and that she is a victim of the 'big girl syndrome'.

Every doctor has met women who cannot lose weight even when they adhere to a strict diet, and they assume the patient is cheating and eating fattening food. This is not necessarily true. There are women, and a percentage of men, whose lack of confidence has reached such proportions that to compensate for their inferiority they over-react and become a domineering person.

It is not sufficient for these people to prove how intelligent they are by becoming leaders in their local community, and self-proclaimed authorities on any subject their friends may happen to be interested in to prove to themselves their own superiority, they have to be physically large as well in order to dominate, by their size, their social and professional fields.

The women with the 'big girl syndrome' have an intense desire to be loved and nurtured that goes back into a childhood where they felt they were rejected. They yearn to find a man who will love them, but frequently their physical proportions are repulsive to the men they meet and with whom they would like to have a permanent relationship. As they often experience the loss of their man, they set about trying to dominate, to 'eat up' and control future men of their choice in order to prevent the rejection. Unfortunately these tactics are unacceptable to most men and they are forced to break off the friendship to have personal freedom.

But irrespective of the reason for obesity, the reason is far more important to the fat man or woman than the fear that their excessive weight will lead to a heart attack.

This became evident during a course for members of the medical and dental professions on psychodynamics and advanced hypno-analytic techniques. A member of the group volunteered to assist the demonstrator because he had become a compulsive eater without knowing why. He was helped to achieve the state known as hypnosis, and by various techniques his problem was unearthed, in the same way a jig-saw puzzle is put together, piece by piece. It transpired he had been a heavy cigarette smoker until his father had died in agony as the result of cancer of the lung, and as the experience had been traumatic for the volunteer he had decided he would become a non-smoker.

That was part of the picture. The other section had its roots in the Second World War when he had been in the Armed Forces serving in the Far Eastern theatre of operations. At one time in his military career he had been on an operation behind Japanese enemy lines, when he and other members of the same unit had virtually no food for two weeks. It was then, while he was starving, he made a personal vow that he would never again, as long as he lived, place himself in a position where he could not get enough to eat.

The Second World War episode gave him a predisposition to over-eating which he explained as, 'I am really a human camel! I am storing up food inside me in case I should meet another situation where I cannot get enough to eat.'

On the surface his explanation was logical, but obviously there was more to it than that. For if it had been the complete answer, why did he not put on weight at the end of the war, and what had his father's death from cancer got to do with his problem?

Hypno-analysis was continued until he was able to provide the complete answer, which was: 'Having seen my father die such a horrible death due to his smoking, I decided I would stop smoking and eat, because this means I will not die of cancer of the lungs, but of a coronary which is much more preferable.'

To avoid one form of death, cancer, he was deliberately seeking another, coronary thrombosis, and he was unaware of the fact that a small but increasing number of eminent members of the medical profession accept that cancer is a psychosomatic illness which attacks those who feel that life has failed them by not providing all they had hoped it would, or that they have failed life by not achieving those things they knew they should and could have achieved.

Admittedly the idea of cancer being psychosomatic, yet another stress disease, is unacceptable to the majority of doctors

44

and the general public even though there is mounting evidence to show the causal relationship. The usual response to this concept is an emotive antagonism, and Dr Lawrence LeShan, PhD, a well known American psychologist who has made an extensive study of the link between emotions and cancer, gave one of his experiences of the illogicality to members of the Association for the Advancement of Psychoanalysis at the New York Academy of Medicine on 27 May 1964.

After a paper on the 'Irrational Complications of the Cancer Problem' had been read by Dr Gotthard Booth, MD, of New York City, there was a discussion, and Dr LeShan told how, in 1952, he arrived in New York with a monetary grant to research into this area.

He said he had approached twelve of the leading hospitals for facilities to carry out the research programme, but none of them were interested. The attitude of the hospital administrators was, 'We do not care to be associated with this type of research,' and a leading surgeon told LeShan, 'Even if you prove in ten years that there is a relationship between personality and cancer, I won't believe it.'[7]

The primary reason for this sort of emotionalism and unscientific rejection of available data is that it is unpalatable to the intellect to accept that a man or woman, any of us, can create within themselves a disease which is malignant and, at present, frequently fatal. It is more pleasant to believe the human body is invaded by an alien virus, which can be studied under the microscope and fought by medical and pharmacological technology, and accept that if the invading host should win the final battle between life and death, this is part of the natural law of survival.

But what facts are available to support the theory that cancer may be psychosomatic? There has been, and still is, a widespread publicity campaign in Britain and the United States showing the correlation between lung cancer and cigarette smoking, and both countries have now legislated that the cigarette manufacturers print on each package a warning that smoking can damage your health, but there is no explanation forthcoming to explain why 10–20 per cent of all lung cancer patients in the United States

[7] *The American Journal of Psychoanalysis*, Vol. XXV, No. 1.

have never smoked,[8] and more than 40 per cent of the lung-cancer deaths in Switzerland cannot be traced to cigarette smoking.[9]

Although the governmental agencies may prefer to ignore this anomaly, the work of the late Dr David M. Kissen, MD, Director of the Psychosomatic Research Unit at Southern General Hospital, Glasgow, may shed some light. He came to the conclusion, after making a depth study of patients suffering from cancer of the lung, that the personality of the patients was more important than the fact they had been smokers, and it was their personality which prevented them from releasing the tension arising through problems in their personal life, 'disturbed marital relationships, poor relationships with parents and children, failure to gain promotion at work, and sexual difficulties'.[10]

He also presented the rather startling observation, supported by Sir Ronald Fisher in his book *Smoking: The Cancer Controversy*[11] that lung cancer patients had the same type of personality, irrespective of the countries they lived in, and smoking and the inhalation of tobacco may well tend to ward off experiences of frustration which might lead to the development of cancer.[12]

If what Kissen and others have said is correct, then the British and American governments' crusade against cigarette smoking is off on the wrong tack, and instead of saving lives it may be creating more tension within potential lung-cancer victims, which in turn, must lead to an increase, rather than a decrease, in lung cancer statistics!

[8] US Surgeon General, *Smoking and Health*, US Public Health Service, Washington, DC, 1964.

[9] T. Abelin, 'Cancer and Smoking in Switzerland: Analysis of All Patients Who Died of Lung Cancer in Switzerland, 1951–1969', *Schw. Med. Wschr.*, 95: 253, 1965.

[10] David M. Kissen, 'Relationship between Lung Cancer, Cigarette Smoking, Inhalation and Personality', *British Journal of Medical Psychology*, 37: 203, 1964; and *The Observer*, 22 January 1967.

[11] Published by Oliver & Boyd, Edinburgh and London, 1959.

[12] See *Psychosocial Aspects of Lung Cancer* presented by Dr Gotthard Booth, MD, at the Fourth International Psychosomatic Cancer Study Group, Turin, Italy, 9–13 June 1965.

As I am a layman this may be an affront to the medical pundits, that I have the audacity to challenge them, but I am not alone in this. A British psychiatrist, Dr Alan McGlashan, wrote in *The Lancet*,[13] that the way to good health is not through watching what is eaten, drunk or smoked, 'It is anxiety, not tobacco or coffee or softwater, that is the hidden destroyer of the contemporary world.' And he urged his colleagues to be more aware of the danger of causing anxiety by their announcements and actions, and said more time and money should be spent on medical research into ways of decreasing, instead of increasing, the anxiety level.

An internationally acknowledged expert on personality and cancer, Dr Gotthard Booth,[14] said in the course of delivering his paper 'Prevention and Cure of Cancer' to the National Federation of Spiritual Healers in Manchester, England, on 29 April 1972, that the personality of the cancer patients is 'characterized by single-minded devotion to circumscribed, unchanging objectives. This makes them self-sufficient and successful until they lose the person or work to which they have attached themselves. If they experience the loss as irretrievable, they become desperate and produce cancer cells.'

Later in the same paper Dr Booth continued:

In his state of despair, the cancer-prone person turns away from the world and *unconsciously* satisfies his need for control by creating an object which cannot be taken from him without his consent – the cancer. That the cancer fulfils a vital need is evident from the observation that *the tumour develops in the organ which has expressed his most important need*. The most obvious examples are provided by cancers of the sexual organs. Cancers of the womb are most frequent when women can no longer have children, cancers of the cervix of the womb, and the prostate when there is no hope of finding a congenial mate. We must understand, however, that the body organs have not only physical,

[13] Issue dated 9 October 1971.
[14] Dr Booth obtained his MD at the University of Munich in 1923; is a Fellow of the American Psychiatric Association; Member of the American Psychosomatic Society; Charter Fellow of the International Psychosomatic Cancer Study Group; Research Assistant of the New York Psychiatric Institute 1951–61; Past President of the Schilder Society for Psychotherapy and Psychopathology; and a member of the Committee on Medicine and Religion of the American Medical Association.

but also symbolic meaning. The breasts for instance, express the need for nursing in the wider sense of the word. Breast cancers therefore develop in mothers whose children have become independent, but also in women who never had children, like nurses, nuns and school teachers who experienced frustration in taking care of the sick and of the educational needs of youth.

Back in 1942 the late Dr Wilhelm Reich noted that repression of highly-charged emotions plays an important role in the precancerous person, and he laid emphasis on the patient's inability to let go in the sexual embrace – that they had poor sexual outlets.[15] The result is that certain parts of the body are kept in a state of tension, and the continual strain in the area prevents the free flow of oxygen, leading to cancer there. Nor is this wildly speculative, because laboratory experiments have shown Reich's ideas to be based upon fact.

Otto Warberg witnessed embryonic chicken cells turned into highly malignant cancers when they were deprived of oxygen, and then return to normal within two days once the supply of oxygen had been restored.

Here it could be argued that these are still only observations, and a demand made, 'Where is the evidence?'

Part of the answer has already been given in Chapter One with my quoting Thomas H. Holmes and Minoru Masuda from *Psychology Today*: 'There was a highly significant correlation between life-change scores and chronic disease (leukemia, cancer, heart attack, schizophrenia, menstrual difficulties and warts)'.

Further empirical evidence is provided by cancer patients themselves. Medical annals are full of reports on spontaneous remission of cancer; when a patient has had the cancer diagnosed and confirmed as 'incurable', but instead of dying, recovers completely, and upon further investigation is pronounced free from any malignancy.

These cases, and there are large numbers of them, *prove* that the body has the power, within itself, to destroy the cancer should it desire to do so. What gives the patient the *desire* to return to good health is now being studied by the psychosomatic

[15] Wilhelm Reich, *Selected Writings*, Noonday Press, New York, 1961.

researchers, so the mechanisms involved can be understood and repeated to assist other victims.

But let us look at individuals, like the young lady who had only been married for a short time, and was emotionally dependent upon her husband as a father-figure. When he left her for another woman she rapidly developed cancer of the cervix, and her unconscious motivation for producing the malignancy in the reproductive area was to punish herself for her own sexual inadequacy – she had never had an orgasm – as she was sure if their sex life had been better he would not have needed an extra-marital relationship. So she tried to destroy her sexuality by cancer of the cervix. She was lucky. She ceased to dwell upon the loss and altered her life-style completely. The result being, she has been cancer free for more than the prescribed five years which medically denotes a cure.

Two other interesting cases were mentioned by Dr Vivian A. Tenney, MD, during a discussion following the reading of a paper on 'Spontaneous Regression of Cancer' by Dr Gotthard Booth.

Dr Tenney related how a woman with cancer of the uterus was seen by the surgeon due to operate upon her. The patient appeared to be willing to talk about herself and her life to the surgeon, and she assured him that she had been happy. But when Dr Tenney spoke to her husband he gave a different picture. Their son had been a trial to them both. 'He has embezzled money, forged cheques, borrowed from our friends. I have tried everything,' the father said, 'set him up in business which he failed in, paid off his debts, and spent $100,000 to keep him out of jail. I think this worry has a lot to do with my wife's cancer.'

The interpretation Dr Tenney made was, 'The sarcoma was in the uterus which had nurtured this child. The grief and bitterness caused by her son, had revealed itself in the organ most closely related to him. It was as though she were saying "By giving birth to you, I gave birth to an evil, malignant being who has ruined my life". She could not admit this consciously, of course, so she dammed it down into her subconscious and ten years later the secret of "what was eating her" emerged in the physical sarcoma. She was found to be inoperable.'

A doctor had carcinoma of the bowel, and after an operation when the growth was not removed, he was sent home to die. Some of his medical colleagues asked the patient if he would write a paper on his reactions to being stricken by cancer, and the knowledge that the prognosis was poor.

Initially the doctor felt the task was beyond him, but his son and daughter-in-law, both physicians, urged him to do it. He started, and was soon so engrossed in the work that what started out as a paper began to emerge as a book. As the book took shape, his health improved. After its publication, and the good reviews it received, he decided he was fit enough to return to full time medical practice, where he worked for five years, dying of a coronary at the age of seventy-six. According to Dr Tenney, 'He found a reason for living and felt valued and loved and needed.'

I could go on quoting case after case showing where the build up of anxiety-tension-stress plays a determining part in a continuum of illnesses, ranging from the common cold, through infertility in women, to cancer at the other extreme. But in the final analysis they all tend to confirm that perhaps Dr Georg Groddeck was right after all when he proclaimed that all illness was a manifestation of the unconscious mind trying to find, by a child-like logic of its own, an answer to the problem currently confronting it.

Chapter 3
The social germs

Once it is accepted that stress disease is on the increase, the next step is to examine the environment to ascertain what is happening in that sphere, and to try to isolate the social germs which are contributing to the epidemic. To do this it is equally necessary to review the basic needs of men and women, because this will reveal where and when these are compatible with society, and where they are being frustrated.

Starting at the beginning, the human needs food, water and warmth for physical survival, but there is more to living than that, and to enjoy life the human needs to be loved, wanted and accepted; to be recognized for his or her individuality, and above all, as no one is an island unto himself, a need to be in contact, and able to communicate with other people.

In an effort to get the desired recognition children will show off and put on an act at times, and this is particularly noticeable when visitors arrive at their home. If the child then feels he is being ignored – something none of us like to happen – he will get up to an antic, even being a downright nuisance and getting punished, to gain attention.

A mother may be taking her small daughter shopping and meet a friend outside the supermarket. If she stops talking too long her daughter will grab hold of her hand saying, 'Come on, Mummy, I want to go.' She does not necessarily want to go home. What she does want is attention. And if that strategy does not work the little girl will think of a dozen more ways to try, like climbing on a nearby wall and balancing on one leg, then shouting out, 'Mummy, watch me. Watch me'. She is aware that what she is doing could be dangerous. That is why she is doing it. But she also knows Mummy will react, either by leaving her friend to rescue her, or by drawing her friend's attention to her daughter and commenting, 'She has a remarkable sense of balance, and we are sure she is going to be a dancer', or 'She is a real tomboy, not at all ladylike. I don't know what she will be like when she grows up.' It does not matter what her mother says, as long as she says something, for that is the reward.

As children grow up and become adults they alter the games they play to gain attention and to stand out from the crowd, but they still play them. It might be the car they have or the way they drive it; it might be the clothes they wear or their hair styles; their house, the way it is furnished; their use of language; the job they do; currying favour with the boss. The games vary, but they are all ways of seeking personal recognition.

Of course there is nothing novel in my assessment of human needs. Governments recognize it, and issue platitudinous statements about 'the sacred rights of the individual' which they promise to uphold. Wars are fought for it, and when that happens the first thing to be sacrificed by the warring nations is the very thing they are allegedly fighting for. Politicians seeking office use it as a catch-phrase to solicit votes, and the electorate continues hoping that one day a miracle will occur and the elected candidate will remember their needs.

But having defined them, let us take a look and see how they fit into the reality of modern technological society.

The popular notion is that women suffer more from psycho-neurotic conditions, such as phobias and depression, and men are more prone to psychosomatic illnesses, like coronaries. Whether this is correct is unimportant, but as the mental well-being and good health of women affects the males they are in contact with, it appears to me to be pertinent that the life-style of the female should take precedence.

Not all that long ago, within my own life time in the United Kingdom, urbanization was in its infancy, and it was rare for a family to move away from the village or town where they were born to find work or advancement.

If anyone did leave to go to college or university it was the unwritten law that they returned home once they had qualified.

People were born in an area, married someone who lived in the vicinity, and set up home there. And this was, and still is, important as it meant that when the husband was at work the wife was not isolated from those near and dear to her. She could, and did, go and visit her parents, aunts, uncles, cousins and the many friends she had grown up with. They could talk and share confidences. When they were worried there was someone to talk to. And when she went shopping she knew the local shopkeepers, and could pass the time of day with them. She met her friends in the same shops and there was security in belonging to a community.

Nor was this confined to rural communities. In towns and large cities there was the same cohesiveness and contact within the district where the people resided. If a girl worked before and after her marriage, the possibilities were she had a job in a small office belonging to a local businessman; in a store which was personally supervised by the owner; or in a local factory owned by the same family for generations. She knew the boss, and there was a sense of purpose in her work.

Should a husband decide the time had come for him and his family to move from their native locality because he wanted to improve himself, it was a personal decision. He was not forced into moving, for even unemployment was not a deciding factor. If the town or village had a high unemployment rate, then he and all the men he had grown up with were sharing a common experience.

The adventurous could be absorbed into the vast under-populated empire which the British still possessed, and in the United States the size of the nation allowed a similar freedom of movement.

Now let us look at what is happening to the modern woman. A major difference is that today she is better educated at an intellectual level, her mind trained to be active. But most of the jobs available to her are boring, monotonous and frustrating.

She lives on a housing estate where the largest number of houses are built within the smallest amount of space, and usually some distance from where she was born and raised. Her relatives and former friends have shared the same fate which has deprived all of them of someone to talk to.

The local stores, if they are still operating instead of being replaced by impersonal supermarkets, have been forced to adopt a self-service format where there are no friendly assistants to exchange the time of day. And if a neighbour happens to be in the store at the same time it is impossible to stop and talk without causing a shoppers-jam due to the amount of goods stacked on row after row of shelves.

For the female worker conditions have also altered to her detriment. The invisible presence of time and motion study engineers has pervaded even the smallest office where conversation and inter-personal communication is limited to the bare minimum, and the typist, once the elite worker, has become an extension of her typewriter, working in typing pools with the work being taken to her and collected afterwards.

In the factories the same depersonalized approach is applied, although in one of them it was carried through to the point of absurdity when a woman, complete with stop-watch was stationed in the ladies' lavatory to keep a record of the users, the number of times they answered nature's call in a day, and the duration. If the visits to and the time spent in the lavatory were considered to be excessive, the management warned the offender.

Increasing the depersonalization is the growth of large financial combines where the workers have no contact with their employers and policies which affect them are decided in distant head offices by unknown administrators. The women workers, and the men too, see themselves as pawns to be manipulated by unseen chess-players who have no interest in them as individuals, but only in the profits recorded by some equally unknown accounts department.

At the end of the day the women are freed from the enforced lack of contact, to return home. But what happens there? On goes the television and communication is again curtailed.

For the married woman alone all day in her insular semi-detached house there are labour saving machines to help her get through the household chores quickly, leaving her spare time with nothing to fill it. Agreed she may have children, but as much as she may love them they cannot fill the mental stimulation and communication void.

When all this is put together it explains why bingo halls are so popular with married women. The game fills two needs; a chance to emerge from the isolation of their homes, to meet people, to talk and be an integral part of a group sharing a common interest, and it gives them a chance to be seen as an individual, because when they win the spotlight is on them.

Those who live in high-rise apartment buildings are faced with even greater isolation, and there have been cases where inmates of these concrete pinnacles have died, and their deaths remained undiscovered for days afterwards.

The children in the concrete jungles are also affected. Research has shown they can become educationally disadvantaged through the lack of opportunity to play with other children, and this retards language development, so that when they go to school they have difficulties in learning to read. (Of course this is but one of the reasons for the high proportion of poor readers. Another is that television has replaced conversation in the home between parents, and among brothers and sisters. The TV has also replaced books to a degree as an audio-visual escape from restricting reality, making the written word more tedious.)

No one knows where this is going to end as the mammoth businesses continue to attract more and more people into an urbanized existence, uprooting families and settling them in functionally ideal suburbs, and in houses that are identical, thereby increasing the feeling of isolation and loss of personal identity.

We may not know where the end will be, but animal experiments, particularly with rats, have shown what happens when overcrowding reaches a certain level. The initial reaction is to try and find another, less crowded space, and when this is unsuccessful due to the confinement of the cage – in men and women the confinement would be the cage of employment – aggressive tendencies make a positive appearance as they begin to resort to violence. Finding no relief in aggression the rats become withdrawn, uncommunicative, and there is an increase in homosexuality among the males, and a loss of interest in the babies by the females.

While I am more than ready to agree that experiments conducted with rats cannot necessarily be applied to humans, it does not mean we can dismiss them out of hand, because the same manifestations are now appearing in our towns and cities.

Every doctor, psychiatrist and psychotherapist is aware of the price people are having to pay for this lack of contact and communication. They know that their patients suffering from stress-disorders are really looking for someone who will acknowledge and accept them as an individual; someone who will listen to them and try to understand their problems. Give them what they want and they begin to feel better. But who is going to give it to them? The overworked doctors? Some have tried, and found themselves in an awkward position, for once they have allowed the verbal lockgates to be opened there is such a welter of things to be said that the patient becomes rather a pest as they have no one else to turn to.

According to Dr Gotthard Booth the worker's inability to escape from his urbanized trap plays a part in both lung cancer and asthma.[1]

He states that the lungs are closely associated with mankind's development and capacity for freedom, as it was the lungs which enabled animal life, from which we evolved, to leave the sea and live on land, and breathe air. 'The emigration of organisms from the water was the crucial step which led to the emergence of man, to his freedom of choosing a habitat anywhere on earth.' At the moment of birth the baby re-enacts the historical event as it takes its first breath of air after emerging from the liquid surrounding it as a foetus, and that marks the dawn of its independence from the mother.

Dr Booth adds, 'Everybody, no matter how old, continues to respond with a deep breath to the experience of liberation from a physically or psychologically confining situation.' And Drs T. M. French and F. Alexander, in their published findings relating to bronchial asthma, say that the attacks occur when there is a conflict between a need for personal freedom on the one hand, and a fear of failure on the other.[2]

However, Booth has a more important comment to make about the worker who is restricted.

The increase in lung cancer is *much higher in men than in women*. This

[1] Gotthard Booth, MD, *Psychosocial Aspects of Lung Cancer*, 1965.
[2] *Psychogenic Factors in Bronchial Asthma*, Vol. 2, Psychosomatic Medicine Monographs, Washington, 1941.

is in keeping with the fact that in all countries men are subjected to greater stress than women where achievement of independence is concerned. Men work generally under conditions which they control to a very limited extent, married women have in their homes considerable independence and for working women the psychological expectations are generally less ambitious. . . . Viewed in this light, cancer appears as a specific risk for those personalities who are identified with the individualistic society, but frustrated by the contingencies of personal endowment and socio-economic limitations. . . . Lung cancer too is more frequent among those who moved from rural into urban regions than among the native urban population. This applies equally to smokers and non-smokers.

To be fair, it is not only the lower paid workers who experience this frustration. There are many examples of talented and wealthy men whose ambitions have outstripped their potential or opportunities, and if they interpret the limitation as a personal defeat, they become medically at risk.

What Gotthard Booth did not mention is that parents of male children contribute to their eventual frustration by trying to drive a child to fulfil the dreams they have not realized. This is particularly marked in the field of education, where parents urge their children to obtain academic success with, 'You have got to do well at school, because without a good education you will never amount to anything. And your mother and I are determined you will get more out of life than we have done, due to my lack of schooling.' Their desire to give their children a sound basis for future success is understandable, but it can be psychologically dangerous.

A schoolboy in Britain recently took his 'O' level examinations in ten subjects, and on the day the results were published he was found in a state of mental collapse in a field behind the school. He had got top marks in nine out of the ten subjects, and a good pass-mark in the tenth, but he felt he had let his parents down.

Equally plans for the future, daydreams, are vital to continued good health, and once these are lost, and the future is without hope, ill-health and death begin to loom on the horizon.

This became evident with a gentleman in his sixties who had built up a national organization from nothing. As his retirement drew near, and the younger members of the board of directors wanted to take over the reins, he had three severe heart attacks. He lost the ability to sleep, and developed an oedema, or dropsy (an accumulation of water in the tissues). A cardiac specialist was consulted to ascertain his chances of survival. They were nil, and the specialist's prognosis was that death was inevitable in view of the condition of the patient's heart.

More to ease his few remaining days than to assist in a cure, a psychotherapist was called in to see if he could help the patient to relax, and it was purely by accident the therapist learned that the man in question would have been offered, if he had not had the heart attack, a coveted public appointment. According to the patient's wife, her husband saw the offered appointment as the crowning achievement of his life, and was very disappointed when he learned that the specialist said it was out of the question, because the strenuous duties involved would place an unbearable burden upon his already weakened heart.

Armed with that knowledge the therapist decided he had to take a chance. He told the wife, 'Your husband has got to have a reason to live if he is going to recover. If he hasn't got one then I'm sure my efforts will be in vain. Therefore, with your permission, I am going to encourage him to get well so that he can take up the appointment when it is offered to him. I know this may sound cruel, because he might die before that. But, at least, he will die a happy man. Have I your permission to put this into practice?'

Through talking with the therapist and making plans for the future, combined with skilful medical care and treatment, the patient realized that relaxation could unlock the door to the future for him. His improvement was rapid, and when he was finally offered the appointment he was able to accept it. For the following year he fulfilled long and arduous duties without any reoccurrence of cardiac failure, and today, many years later, he is still alive and involved in living.

The key to the successful outcome of this therapeutic approach, if there was one, was the wife's consent to also encourage her husband to get well so that his dream would become a reality. If she had not agreed the outcome could have been quite different, as the therapist found a few weeks later.

Obviously pleased with the results the psychotherapist had obtained, the doctor telephoned him to ask if he would see another man who was unable to relax after a comparatively minor coronary. The therapist could find nothing to revitalize the new patient and to make matters worse the patient's wife seemed to be more concerned about her future than that of her husband.

Every time he called she was emphasizing, in her husband's presence, how difficult the future was going to be. She would turn to her husband and say, 'Of course you won't be able to carry on as you did before dear, once you get better. You will have to retire, won't you?

'This will make a great difference to our lives,' she said, turning to the therapist. 'Of course, we shall survive, but this lovely house will have to go, won't it dear?' Her husband lay in bed, ignoring the question. Despite the therapist's remonstrations, nothing could dissuade her from voicing her pessimism, and while the coronary thrombosis had not been severe, the patient had a second cardiac attack and died.

Insurance companies who underwrite pension schemes are fully aware that once a man feels he is no longer useful, and has nothing more to contribute, they will not have to continue paying his pension for long.

The fact that many men see retirement as being synonymous with the end of a useful life was understood by a large manufacturing company in Britain owned by a family of Quakers, and the employers took positive steps to prevent this from happening. In their company nobody had to retire. If a man or a woman wanted to work there was always something found for them to do. How long they worked was left to the individual, and they were paid accordingly. Yet the most important thing was and is, that they were made to feel needed and that they could still make a contribution.

Not all companies are this concerned. Most are too big and complex, with their workers a cypher on a graph, and while they provide fringe benefits, distribute newsletters and magazines, the entire operation is impersonal. The jobs the workers do are impersonal, and the amount of job-satisfaction is negligible.

An examination of the system employed in a large factory

where there is a production line highlights the problem facing the industrial working man. All unnecessary movement has been carefully eliminated so that the work-flow is uninterrupted. Conversation is limited by the restriction of physical movement, and often the noise level is a further deterrent.

Making matters worse, the job-performance of each man has been analysed so that from the moment he starts work to the time he finishes he repeats, at timed intervals, the same monotonous task. This is destructive, and saps a man's dream of the future.

As youngsters entering the factory the dreams were there, that they would learn their trade, and then move on to better things. These hopes were unearthed by a television reporter talking to workers at the main Rolls-Royce factory when it was faced with closure. The interviewer asked them why they had not left, and carried out their plans. The answers he received all spoke of the same traps: 'I got married and then there were the children . . .' 'There was the mortgage of the house . . .' 'My wife and I talked about making a move in the early days, we both wanted to then, but . . .' And so the men who once had fine dreams for the future no longer dreamed. They were bitter and disillusioned, and if they heard a young apprentice talking about his hopes for the future they forgot they had the same visions when they were his age, and instead of encouraging the boy to make his dreams a reality, they bitterly said, 'Why don't you start to grow up. You will still be here when you are old enough to draw your pension.'

On an executive level some companies adopt policies which are designed to ensnare their senior workers. The idea of the 'company man' which was developed in the United States was geared to providing everything a man and his wife may require. Free and private medical, dental and hospital services; a company club; a host of organized hobbies and sports activities; a company house with company-assisted financing to buy the furniture and a car. Once the executive was caught in those meshes he only had one fear. The threat of losing his job!

It proved to be a costly experiment, because the men would not take decisions in case they were wrong, and the mistake jeopardized their future. But the concept is still very much alive in many countries, and if the company has not adopted the programme in its entirety, the inflated salaries and fringe benefits achieve the same objective.

I talked to a thirty-one-year-old man who had just been made the managing director of a prosperous organization, and asked him how he felt about his appointment. He expressed his pleasure, but qualified it by adding that he was more anxious than he had ever been, because he knew that unless he produced the results expected of him, he would be replaced. 'And, Peter, I have no idea where I would get another job with the same salary, and I need the money now, due to the new commitments I have.'

A sales manager with an excellent record was asked one morning to see the chairman of the board of directors. He had no idea why the boss wanted to see him, and it was with some trepidation he went to his office. He was asked to sit down, then he was informed that his work had been noted by the directors, and it was their unanimous decision that, from that moment, he was promoted to being the sales director with an increase in salary, and that a new car, more appropriate to his new position, was waiting for him on the forecourt.

The man walked out in a happy daze, but two days later he entered a depressive state requiring prolonged psychotherapy. While he was in analysis the reason for his depression was unearthed. He felt he had sacrificed his freedom, and as the sales director he would be completely committed to the job, and the chances of ever changing his life-style had gone forever.

After seeing how the working man's needs are thwarted by the commercial world it is not surprising that the death rate through coronaries is mounting in the forty- to fifty-year-old age bracket, as it is then that the male is most disillusioned, and can see no chance for himself in the future.

It also explains why industry is plagued by strikes as the workers try to obtain from the management recognition that they are not faceless robots, but men and women who, like the former slaves, want to be treated with dignity as human beings.

Additionally, it discloses the origins of the common cold epidemics that annually cause millions of lost working days. For catching a cold is the only way a large number of people can register their protest against the embracing collectivism.

In August 1972 the Office of Health Economics in London issued a report about claims made for sickness benefit payments, and one of the reasons put forward as to why thousands of men and women 'go sick' is that they want to escape from mentally unrewarding jobs.

According to the report the most prevalent reason for absence in men is respiratory disorders, accounting for ninety-three million lost working days in 1969–70, and mental illness for fifty-one million lost days.

Mr William Laing, deputy director of the Office of Health Economics, was quoted in *The Daily Telegraph* newspaper as saying:

The recorded causes of absence tell only part of the story. It is increasingly recognized that conditions like 'bronchitis 'or 'slipped disc' are simply used as convenient diagnostic labels for episodes of absence which often owe more to social and economic factors than a simple inability to work for medical reasons.[3]

I discussed these assertions with a senior executive of an international organization whose conveyor-belt factories are always making newspaper headlines due to the large number of strikes continually affecting them, long before the Office of Health Economics issued its report. He was not surprised at what I said, and he did not try to argue against the points I had raised. On the contrary, he was ready to agree that money had little to do with absenteeism and the strikes, as the workers were in a very highly paid industry.

The cause, according to him, was that work on the production lines was boring due to the monotony of the routine tasks and lack of contact between the men during working hours. But, he continued, his organization had decided it was cheaper to budget for the time lost in strikes and 'illness' than to change the production system.

This final comment startled me. Since the emergence of computers, and the rapid strides made in industrial technology, I had

[3] Issue dated 14 August 1972.

repeatedly read about alert politicians and public spirited citizens voicing their fears that the time could come when these machines could take over, and men would be subservient to them. It struck me then that the watchdogs were too late, and that mankind was already a servant of the machine.

Why did not his organization, and others, plan in-service training so the men would learn to undertake various jobs along the production line, and subsequently be rotated at comparatively short and irregular intervals to prevent the boredom, I enquired?

He admitted the plan sounded plausible, though he was sure it would not work out. Why? I wanted to know. 'It is impractical,' he patiently explained, 'because different jobs have different pay scales, and the trade unions would be bound to object if they were interfered with.'

His argument may have validity, but I still wonder how many men, and what trade union, would be prepared to oppose such a scheme if they knew that by adhering to the present system they were shortening their lives, and the lives of their members?

Chapter 4
The birth of stress

As it is impossible to put the clock back and, like some modern reincarnated King Canute try to stop the onrushing tide of technological progress, the future might look bleak, with men and women already having demonstrated that they are finding it increasingly difficult to cope with the stress life today engenders.

Realizing this dilemma, various questions haunted me. I was aware that anxiety is an innate part of the human make-up, and has been with us since man took his first breath on dry land, so 'Why is this happening?' I asked myself. 'What has happened to man in the last hundred years? What has the *individual* lost which prevents him or her from adapting to the changing world?'

There were no immediate answers, but there was a steady stream of clues provided by the clients I saw. It did not matter what specific symptom they presented, underneath there was a common denominator: they all had the inability to let go, and be themselves, because they were frightened their behaviour would lead to them being rejected or ridiculed.

The man who had to paralyse his right arm to prevent him from attacking his mother for having rejected him as a nine-year-old; the woman who needed to have her stiff neck to prevent her from surrendering to pressure and impulsively permitting sexual intercourse which she knew would be silly as it would endanger her marriage; the man who needed his facial acne to prevent him from giving way to his sexual desires which his parents had told him were wrong; the woman who could not eat or drink in the presence of other people, 'because I might do something foolish . . .'

In addition to their basic fear, when they were in analysis it became patently obvious that the origins lay in their earlier childhood relationships, or lack of relationships, with their parents.

In a small therapeutic group formed to assist overweight women, a lady told her peers that she had become a compulsive eater three years before, and her additional weight had since stopped her from going out with her husband in their leisure hours because 'I am so ugly he wouldn't want to be seen with me.'

No amount of reassurance from members of the group that her appearance was not repulsive had any effect upon her. The self-image she had of herself as a fat and ugly person remained.

'Did anything happen to you three years ago which made you think you were unattractive?' she was asked.

'Yes,' she replied. 'I found out my husband had another woman.'

She paused for a moment, then continued, 'It has always been the same. Everyone I have ever trusted has let me down, so there must be something wrong with me.'

'Surely not,' one of the ladies remonstrated. 'Your parents didn't let you down, did they?'

'Yes they did,' was the quick retort. 'My father died when I was very young, and my mother was always out with other men after that. Then one day she took me to a place I later found out was the welfare office. She told me she was going to the toilet, but I never saw her again, and I was put in an orphanage.'

From that isolated and rather dramatic case it was obvious that the causation of her obesity was not her husband's extra-marital relationship, it had only triggered off the sense of loss of love experienced when her mother rejected her as a child.

However, that and other exceptional examples did not explain why people who had not known the same traumatic rejection had similar reactions.

A partial answer to that came when I found it necessary to regress certain clients through their lives to relive the trauma of their birth before their symptomatology remissed.[1]

An Israeli doctor who had heard of my work was afflicted by a strong presentiment he was going to die as a result of a malignant tumour which was going to develop on the left side of his fore-

[1] See Peter Blythe, *Hypnotism: Its Power and Practice*, Arthur Barker, London, 1971, pages 77–80.

head. Without any prompting on my part, his unconscious mind indicated that the sensitizing event was his birth.

I took him back, under hypnosis, to the time he was born, and gave him the suggestion that he would remember and relive everything that had happened to him as he was being born, and that he would be able to tell me exactly what was happening, and what he was feeling.

He re-enacted his birth process which was prolonged and difficult, both for him and his mother. And at one point he was sure, due to the agony his mother was suffering, she was going to die, and he cried out in anguish, 'I'm killing her. Tell them to stop, because I'm killing her. And she cannot die. I need her.'

Eventually he was delivered by a pair of forceps gripping him hard on the left temporal lobe – the spot where he felt the cancer was going to attack him. But in his unconscious mind the thought had remained that he had tried to kill his mother, and his punishment was to die slowly, as he had been born. It was when he relived taking his first breath, and established a regular breathing pattern he started to laugh. 'I didn't kill her. I didn't even try to, and so I don't have to die.'

This and other cases were a step forward, although they left two aspects of the puzzle still unresolved.

The infant cannot talk when it is born, therefore, when clients verbalize what is happening to them as they relive being born, it is possible they are only acting out what they think happened to them, rather than presenting a true regression. For a time this worried me, until I read the results of research conducted by others.

The work of Dr Wilhelm Reich, and the findings of Trygve Braaty,[2] revealed how, when we are submitted to powerful, external stimuli which we are incapable of accommodating mentally, it is vital for our survival and sanity that the unacceptable emotions are prevented from transmission to the brain by being locked off and repressed into the part of the body where they are most felt, by instantaneous muscular tension. Then, when the tension is eventually released, irrespective of how long afterwards and by whatever means, the formerly repressed emotions

[2] See page 25.

are permitted to reach the brain, and there be interpreted into words.

Dr Arthur Janov, PhD, the Los Angeles clinical psychologist whose primal therapy and book *The Primal Scream*[3] are currently the centre of wide acclaim and bitter controversy, believes all neuroses stem from the 'primal' (infant) pains which are felt, but never expressed. His hypothesis being, all the mentally unregistered pains build up in the body, and until they are released from the body the neuroses will remain. And at a lecture he gave in London in May 1972 he told his audience that he had seen the birth process relived by hundreds of patients in primal therapy.

The other part of the puzzle was that all humans are born, and while a traumatic birth sowed the seeds of future psychological and psychosomatic illnesses, the birth process alone could not account for people failing to cope with stress.

There appeared to be no answer to this until I worked with an American doctor who was incapable of entering into any kind of relationship, be it with another man or a woman. For reasons he could not comprehend, because he wanted to make friends, he found himself trying to alienate himself from everyone who showed signs of liking him.

Even when we first met he tried to get me to reject him by making a verbal, but very personal attack upon me. That I ignored. Using the hypno-diagnostic technique we discovered the root of his problem lay between his being born and his first birthday.

It was not the trauma of birth, nor was it any one specific event. It was a prolonged emotional experience involving his mother.

When he was regressed back to a newly born infant he cried out for his mother to hold him. The cries became screams as he tried to communicate his intense need to be held in her arms, to her breast, so that he would know she really loved him. Most of the time his cries went unanswered, and when she did pick him up and hold him to her there was no warmth in her embrace.

'You stupid bitch,' he screamed, 'hold me properly. You dry tit. You are a dry tit, and there is no love. Love me. Show me you love me.'

[3] Dell Publishing Co., New York, 1970.

The screams slowly subsided as he did not get the reassuring physical contact from his mother. They became a whimper, and then died away completely as he curled himself into a foetal position.

Following the hypnotic session we talked about what had happened, and he saw the significance. By his mother failing to give him the physical contact he required when he wanted it as an infant, the pain he felt at that time remained within him, and stopped him from ever entering into another relationship with a woman in case the horror was reactivated.

He told me how he remembered, as a young boy, he was not able to communicate with his mother, and tried to overcome the loss by establishing a closer contact with his father. That too was unsuccessful as his father belonged to the antiquated school of thought which equated physical contact between males as something unhealthy and according to my client, he was always too busy anyway. Repulsed by his father, his rejection was complete, and subsequently he could never trust a man or woman again.

After that I began to look more closely at the infant-mother relationship, and the conclusions were inescapable: the way children are reared in modern societies ensures that when the child becomes an adult he will be unable to withstand the pressures of anxiety, because he was robbed of security and trust as an infant.

This might appear a startling condemnation, based upon little evidence. Yet the facts are there to support it once the reader knows what to look for.

Because children are being born every second somewhere in the world scant attention is paid to what is happening to the infant. To discover how this might be remedied let us trace a normal, non-traumatic birth. Before the baby is born its world is secure and warm. The womb temperature is approximately thirty-seven degrees Centigrade. At the moment of birth, when the baby emerges from the vaginal canal, it is submitted to a series of shock waves. The entire skin surface of the body, a mass of sensory receivers which has been accustomed to a womb temperature, suddenly finds itself having to contend with a room temperature which is some seventeen degrees Centigrade lower.

And if that were not shock enough for the system, the newly born infant experiences an onslaught of bright light and noise.

One doesn't have to be a baby to appreciate the startling effect a bright light can have on a person who has been sitting in a darkened room when the light is switched on unexpectedly. The entire organism tenses up in alarm.

Next comes the severance of the umbilical cord, and at that moment, while still in a state of shock, the baby finds itself cut off from any contact with its source of life and security, its mother.

What happens next would be unbelievable if it was not a daily occurrence in any maternity section of any hospital. The baby who requires skin contact with the mother to ward off the shock of separation, isolation, heat, light and noise, is separated from the mother, wrapped up tightly, and placed in a cot in another room. It is kept clinically isolated until prescribed times when it is returned to the mother to be fed, and then separated again.

If this inhuman treatment was inflicted upon an animal, large sections of the press and news media would launch a campaign to have the system altered, but as it happens to a *human infant*, inside a hospital, it is accepted without a murmur.

Evidence of infantile needs can be seen in the work of Harry F. Harlow at the University of Wisconsin in 1958 and 1962. Newly born monkeys were separated from their mothers six to twelve hours after being born, and given two substitute mothers. One was made of wire with a feeding bottle strategically placed, and the other surrogate mother was a wooden structure, covered with foam-rubber and terry cloth, but without a feeding bottle.

The object of this series of experiments undertaken by Harlow and his colleagues was to ascertain what was most important to the infants; being fed, or tactile skin contact, the latter being what Harlow referred to as 'warmth'.

The results were crystal clear. Even those monkeys who were fed solely by the *wire-mother* would spend most of their time clinging to the cloth surrogate, and there is a photograph showing an infant monkey clinging to the cloth figure while leaning over to be fed from the wire model.[4]

[4] See Dr Edward J. Murray, *Motivation and Emotion*, Prentice-Hall, Inc., New Jersey, USA, 1964, Fig. 11.

When the baby monkeys were placed in strange or frightening situations they would seek the protection of the cloth mother, but if it had been removed when the threat to them was evoked, the monkeys would shrink into a frozen, crouching position; they would rock themselves backwards and forwards; commence sucking their fingers, and generally producing recognized disturbed, emotional behaviour.

Nor were the effects of separation from the real mother of short duration. The effects lasted for years.

By 1962 Harlow discovered that his monkeys who had been raised with wire mother-figures were unable to express, or be the beneficiary of, affection. They were unco-operative in their adult relationships; were more than normally aggressive; and were unable to engage in normal sexual intercourse, even with monkeys of the opposite sex who were experienced in sexual behaviour.

The other experimental monkeys who had been reared by cloth-mothers were less aggressive in comparison, but more aggressive than those who had been raised naturally, and while they were capable of some sexual activity and response, they showed all the signs of immaturity.

Another discovery was that all the monkeys who had been deprived of physical warmth and cuddling were sexually crippled in adulthood, and very few of the females became pregnant. Those who did conceive, and irrespective of whether they were reared by cloth or wire figures, were incapable of properly taking care of their babies. They ignored them, refused to allow the baby physical contact with them, and beat the babies so savagely that the young had to be taken away from them – a direct analogy of the present wave of human 'battered babies' which is currently reaching alarming proportions!

Of course we humans do not duplicate the Harlow experiments with our children by giving them surrogate mothers. We do not take away all true physical contact, we just limit it. But, from the work of Professor Liddel of Cornell University, it appears that this may be just as injurious.

Working with twin goats, Professor Liddel separated one of

the twins from its mother for a brief period each day, while leaving the other twin in continual contact. Except for the daily experimental period of forty minutes, both kids lived with, and were fed by, their mother.

During the experimental periods the lights were extinguished periodically, an effect known to produce anxiety in goats, and that produced very different behaviour in the twins.

The twin which had been with the mother all the time remained at ease and moved about freely. The isolated kid became 'frozen', and cowered in a corner. And in one of the experiments the isolated kid refused to suckle from its mother, and died after a few days.

Again it could be argued this is animal behaviour and not necessarily applicable to humans. To counter this objection, however, there have been numerous studies completed on children who have been deprived of their mothers, for one reason or another, and they have manifested the same syndrome as Harlow's monkeys. In fact, some of the infants have found this isolation to be so intolerable that they have developed marasmus, a condition which caused them to waste away and die like Liddel's kid.

Dr R. A. Spitz did a comparison study on two homes for young babies. In one of the institutions there was a high mortality rate; the children were prone to illness, and they showed mental and physical retardation. In the second home the children were more alert and active and there were no significant illnesses or deaths.

The hygiene standards and medical care facilities were comparable, but Dr Spitz found that in the home where sickness predominated the children had few toys to play with, the sheets were hung over the sides and bottoms of the cots so the babies could only look at the blank ceiling, and there were few nurses available to give the infants attention. Whereas in the other home there were plenty of toys for each child; the cots allowed them to see what was happening around them and to look out of the windows, and the mothers and girls in the home had little to occupy them, so they spent their time playing with and cuddling the babies.

It was the extra attention and stimulation that made the difference between sickness and good health.[5]

However, let us return to looking further at what happens to the newly born. In Britain the expectant mother is given a booklet at the ante-natal clinic which informs her, when she puts her baby into the cot to sleep, if it cries for a time it is nothing to worry about, and she should let it cry as it will soon realize she is not going to pick it up, and go to sleep.

On the surface this looks to be good advice, yet it ignores the fact that a cry, even in an infant who has no other means of verbal communication, is a call for help, or a protest at its loneliness, and to ignore it can increase the child's anguish to the intolerable level where it is forced, for its own psychological protection, to find refuge from the anxiety, by going to sleep.

Having learned to escape from unpleasantness into sleep as an infant, it is not surprising that millions of adults find themselves going to sleep when they are faced with problems they would rather ignore, while it also provides an insight into the origins of the psychological disturbance, neurasthenia, where the unhappy patient is permanently tired and just wants to sleep continually.

Pediatricians, and other child experts who have repressed all the horrors of their own childhood, have laid down laws as to when a baby should be fed, and the amount of food it should be given. This borders upon irresponsible expertise, because only a baby knows when it needs feeding and this will vary from infant to infant, and if a baby does eat more than it requires and is sick, it does not mean the bottle or breast should be limited. The apparent gluttony is a symptom. The baby has already learned that to get the physical contact it needs, it has to pretend to be hungry, but the hunger is not for food, it is for cuddling warmth.

Once this is understood the compulsive eaters can be seen for what they are – lonely people who were taught by their mothers to eat more food than is necessary as a substitute for an inner sense of loss.

If we want our future generations to escape from the stress plague afflicting us we shall have to re-think our notions of baby-

[5]R. A. Spitz, 'Hospitalism', in *The Psychoanalytic Study of the Child*, Vol. 1, edited by O. Fenichel and others, International Universities Press, 1945.

care. The newly born infant will remain with its mother, and in skin-to-skin contact. As the child grows up it will be carried around in a sling instead of being dumped into a perambulator where its vision is limited, and it is deprived of stimuli. When the child is fed, even if the mother prefers bottle- to breast-feeding, she will bare her bosom so her baby can snuggle up against her.

When these measures are adopted the infant will be given, as his birthright, the basic security on which it can build the future, and it will have proof that it can place its trust in others without constantly expecting to be betrayed.

'No woman could possibly do what you ask all the time,' is the opposition I have met when discussing the proposals. 'It is all right for you, a man, to make suggestions like that, because you won't have to be involved. But my child is too demanding as it is, and I have to have some time to do my housework, and a little time left for myself.'

I am ready to admit that women will have to revise their concept of motherhood immediately after their child is born. Yet does what I propose place too great a demand upon mothers, or am I asking them to enjoy the role of being a fully responding mother? As one who can recall the horrors of thoughtless rejection when a child myself, and as an adult who still reacts to it from time to time, I think what I am really asking is for mothers to be Mothers, with a capital M.

On a more positive level I can tell the mothers who have over-demanding children that, if their children had had the contact needed earlier, this would not happen. To be completely honest, they have created their own Frankenstein!

Dr Gotthard Booth made the following observations during his talk in Manchester, in 1972, on 'Healers Day' organized by the National Federation of Spiritual Healers:

When the infant is frustrated in his needs for affectionate interaction with mother or nurse, he fails to develop basic trust in the power of affection, and becomes anxious for establishing control over objects in a limited sphere of existence. This holds true for all infants, but the consequences are particularly severe for infants born with a particularly intense need for affection. [Those whose birth was traumatic, or whose mother was in a prolonged anxiety state during the pregnancy.] For them, the early experience of an inadequate response from the mother lays the foundation for their subsequent fear of frustration and the later despair in the form of cancer.

In the earlier paper delivered in Italy in 1965 Dr Booth had reminded his medical colleagues that cancer in childhood was formerly a rare event, but had become the second most prevalent cause of death in children between the ages of five and fourteen years, and in his opinion this was due to bottle-feeding replacing breast-feeding.

He had more to say about this when in Manchester:

Until the end of the eighteenth century breast-feeding had been the only successful method of raising babies. So called dry-feeding sometimes was tried in emergencies, but the majority of these babies died. In 1769 Dr William Cadogan commented 'the ancient custom of exposing [babies] to wild beasts, or drowning them, would certainly be a much quicker and humane way of despatching them'. Nevertheless toward the end of the eighteenth century, the beginning of the Industrial Revolution forced mothers to return to the factory after having given birth. Their babies had to be dry-fed by grandmothers, maiden aunts and older siblings. Although in the beginning of this practice most of the babies died, with growing practical experience the survival rate slowly improved. Further progress was made when in 1845 the rubber nipple was invented, and medical science succeeded in making bottle-feeding equal to breast-feeding so far as *survival* is concerned. This point was reached in the last decade of the nineteenth century, and more and more physicians and mothers favoured bottle-feeding above breast-feeding. Nobody suspected that the abandonment of breast-feeding involved *serious risks for the later development* of the surviving infants.

Booth referred here to the psychological risks and the possible later psychosomatic illnesses that could result. What he had no way of knowing when he gave his lecture was that Dr Joan L. Caddell, of the St Louis University School of Medicine in St Louis, Missouri, wrote in the medical journal *Lancet* on 4 August 1972, that the cot-death syndrome which claims more than 1,500 babies a year in Britain, could result 'from magnesium deprivation'.

She elaborated on this by pointing out that baby-food formulas based upon cow's milk had a far lower magnesium-phosphorus ratio than human milk, although the prepared foods had a higher protein, calcium and phosphorus content.

Yet, returning to Booth's presentation:

Theoretically, it is possible to give babies all the affectionate experience they need while bottle-feeding them, but in practice this is often not the case.

Breast-feeding has the advantage of mobilizing mutually complimentary *instincts* in the nursing woman and the baby, which practically guarantee affectionate interplay, except in the case of the mother who is abnormally unresponsive. In all forms of artificial feeding affectionate interplay depends on the conscious motivation of the mother or nurse. This conscious motivation is easily neglected in the cases where the mother or nurse is tired, emotionally disturbed or disinterested. In the last century scientific medicine compounded this risk of bottle-feeding, because physicians became excessively preoccupied with the physical aspects of growth, they assumed babies need nothing but a chemically correct formula, a rigid feeding schedule, protection against germs and colds, and sleep when not being fed, diapered – nappied – or bathed. Cuddling, kissing and playing were expressly discouraged. These spontaneous feminine reactions were considered not only unnecessary, but positively unhygienic and bad for character development. In the United States, nine contraptions were patented which made drinking from the bottle possible without the presence of a human being. Undoubtedly, many mothers defied 'doctor's orders', but there can be no doubt that many others accepted them as gospel truth. . . .

The synchronicity between the decline of breast-feeding and the rising incidence of cancer explains why cancer patients are depression prone, and why additional frustrations in later life lead to despair and cancer.

You may find this explanation of the cancer epidemic difficult to accept. I, myself, felt this way. The facts upon which it is based 'stared me in the face' for seven years before I overcame my inhibitions against facing their logical connection. When I presented my conclusions at medical meetings, nobody offered any criticism, but no physician can be happy with the discovery that modern pediatrics, one of the proud achievements of scientific medicine, has been a major accomplice in the creation of the cancer epidemic. When the rank materialism of the Industrial Revolution disrupted the natural mother-infant relationship, the evil to some extent had been self-limiting.

Subsequently, however, materialistic science turned the inhuman economic necessity into a socially acceptable routine by securing the survival of growing numbers of these infants. This unfortunate development is further aggravated by the fact that it is not easily reversed. Many bottle-fed mothers are instinctively inhibited and therefore handicapped in developing a natural spontaneous relationship with their babies even if they try to breast-feed. Parallel with the cancer epidemic, 'lactation failure' has been spreading throughout the modern world.

As you see, understanding the origin of the cancer epidemic does not provide an easy solution of the problem of *prevention*. Even if all mothers would be willing to breast-feed their babies from now on, many would be incapable due to the fact that they themselves, and in many cases, their mothers had been bottle-fed. Nevertheless, the task of prevention is clearly defined: the infant's first year of life must be humanized as much as possible. Fortunately, in the last 25 years there has been an increasing emphasis on the affectionate needs of babies. Greater efforts have been made to re-introduce breast-feeding, and bottle-feeding mothers are encouraged to make the act an occasion for play, rather than a mere fueling operation. Due to their conditioning, some modern mothers are more comfortable with the bottle than with their breasts, and some babies instinctively reject breasts which are offered in a merely dutiful fashion. As the understanding of infant needs becomes more widespread the cause of cancer prevention will be advanced in future generations. . . .[6]

And prior to leaving this subject raised by Gotthard Booth, it is recognized by medical researchers into the psychosomatic causation of cancer that there is a definite correlation between cancer of the breast and the women who do not breast-feed their babies, or who do so for a minimum period of time. Therefore the practice of mechanical bottle-feeding places the non-nursing mother at risk as well as the infant.

It would also be remiss to leave the impression that only babies suffer from separation anxiety. James and Joyce Robertson of the Tavistock Institute in London made a documentary film entitled *John* which showed, without any unnecessary dramatics, what happened to a seventeen-month-old boy who was placed in a

[6] Emphases added by Dr Booth, MD. A copy of his complete address is available from The National Federation of Spiritual Healers, 'Shortacres', Church Hill, Loughton, Essex.

residential nursery for nine days while his mother was in hospital having another baby.[7]

Upon his arrival in the nursery he was a cheerful child, interested in the other five children who lived there permanently. But the ninth day, when his mother arrived to collect him, he would not go near her, and let her pick him up. He had completely withdrawn from human contact and the Robertsons in their follow-up found that his mother could not introduce him to the new baby for six weeks, and after months had elapsed he would become acutely distressed if he was reminded of the period he spent in residential care.

As the same thing occurs when a child goes into hospital, the message which the film conveys is that one nurse should be responsible for looking after the boy or girl, and not a procession of different people, as that increases the lack of security.

In addition to the maternal deprivation, parents insidiously teach their children to be non-people. For the sake of convenience let us create a mythical little boy called Robert of five years who is, in reality, a composite of all small boys and girls. Robert is constantly told, in one way or another, 'You must always tell the truth. To lie is wrong, and if you tell lies Mummy and Daddy won't love you.'

When he does something wrong, and tries to deny he is responsible, he is urged to be honest. 'Now tell us the truth, darling. We won't punish you if you tell us what really happened. What hurts us most of all is when you lie to us.'

This is admirable, but what happens when the boy tells the truth and it is not acceptable? Using our imagination further, perhaps an overbearing relative, an Aunt Minnie, comes to visit at his home, and Robert is told to greet her with a big kiss. 'No, I won't', is Robert's reaction, because he does not like her.

Again he is exhorted to 'give her a kiss, and be a nice little boy,' although this time there is a touch of anger in his father's voice. He remembers what he has been told about honesty, and attempts to explain why he does not want to. 'Daddy, I don't like her. She is fat, and she smells nasty.'

[7] The film *John* can be hired from Concord Films Council, Nacton, Ipswich, Suffolk.

Now his father gets really angry, 'Robert! I don't want any more of that. Go over to your Aunt Minnie immediately and apologize. Give her a kiss, and tell her you didn't mean what you said.'

Dad waits to see how Robert will act, and seeing some hesitation adds, 'Do what I tell you, instantly, or I will send you to bed for the remainder of the day.' Much rather than incur parental displeasure, Robert forces himself to deny his own feelings, and does what is asked of him.

This is only one of many such incidents the boy is subjected to, and he quickly learns to differentiate between what he would like to do and say, and what is acceptable to his parents. So, he conditions himself to always trying to please instead of being himself.

His parents fail to appreciate that their child is a unique individual in his own right and try to mould him into being a reflection of themselves.

By the time he becomes a teenager Robert cannot establish an honest, meaningful relationship with a girl in case she rejects him, and he starts acting in a way which, he hopes, the girl will find acceptable.

Roberta has been through the same non-person process and acts for exactly the same reason, with the outcome that neither partner has the remotest idea of the other's real character. Hence the popular adage, 'You don't really know anyone until you have lived with them for a time.'

Robert and Roberta find employment, but they are still always trying to please. They cannot accept the truism, 'Some people will like you, others will dislike you, and the majority are just not interested.'

If their individual acts are rewarded by recognition from the boss, and they are promoted, the fear of letting the real and submerged self break through, thus shattering the boss's image of them, causes increasing stress. Then if the catastrophe happens and a colleague receives a promotion they wanted, even though they may not have the necessary attributes to fill the vacant position, the false self-concept they have surrounded themselves with collapses, and they either go into a physical or mental decline, or become embittered and antagonistic failures.

Should their role playing be ignored by their employers, they still have the need to find acceptance so they alter their act to fit in with what their workmates expect. This accounts for the herd instinct which is prevalent in industrial strikes. It does not matter to Robert and Roberta whether they agree with the grievances motivating the strike call, they are simply too frightened to voice their own thoughts, because if they behaved contrary to the over-all consensus of opinion they would suffer the all too familiar rejection, and loss of their role.

These two mythical people whose crippled life-style we have just followed are the embodiment of all the clients I have seen, with all their diverse symptoms, because as I wrote at the beginning of the chapter, 'They all had the inability to let go, and be themselves, because they were frightened their behaviour would lead to them being rejected or ridiculed.'

Chapter 5
'Der Führer Prinzip'

It was Dr Leonard M. Cohen, DSSc, of Kingsville, Texas, who told me the theories underlying his 'therapy of logical choices', and the method he used to implement the actual therapy.

As a result of years in practice as a clinical psychologist in the United States, Israel and Britain, Dr Cohen found his patients' heightened state of anxiety made it impossible for them to think logically, and to recall and define the situation which was the basic cause of their tension. This he concluded was a type of escape mechanism; a self-imposed mental and physical amnesia the patient had to maintain to stop himself from thinking about the predicament he had found himself in.

Once he had reached and proven the validity of the role of anxiety, Cohen had to use a therapeutic technique which would lead the patient back to the problem, and he discovered a mirror form of counselling was the most efficient method.

I had the opportunity to sit in with Dr Cohen and a patient to see how it worked. The female patient had been receiving regular medical attention for her nerves for a number of years, and was clearly apprehensive when the three of us met, something which is quite normal when a therapist and patient meet for the first time, yet my presence obviously did not help. However, after telling her that I was another therapist, Dr Cohen proceeded to ignore me, and said to her, 'It is obvious that you have a problem, otherwise you would not be getting the symptoms that you have. Am I correct in surmising that you do have a problem?'

'Oh yes,' she answered emphatically, and without any hesitation.

'That's good. It shows we are off to a good start in our working together,' he said, congratulating her, and at the same time giving her encouragement. 'Would you like to talk about your problem?'

She became confused, and remained silent for a long time, looking backwards and forwards from Dr Cohen to myself, waiting for one of us to break the silence. Neither of us said a word, because the doctor had warned me such a circumstance may arise, and if either of us were to speak, or even make an unnecessary movement, it would give the patient an opportunity to evade answering the question.

Eventually after a lot of fidgeting and the silence had become almost unbearable, she said, 'Not really, Dr Cohen. It is very personal.'

'OK. You say it is "very personal", and I accept that, but why is it very personal?'

'Well, it is about my husband.'

'It is about your husband! What about your husband?'

'He wants a divorce,' was her reply.

'He wants a divorce?' the doctor said, repeating her own words in the form of a question. But when she looked blankly at him, as if she had not understood what he meant, he asked, 'Why does he want a divorce?'

She gave him the reasons, and by mirroring her own words continually back to her, he quickly got her to define her entire problem.

Yet the patient's overt symptomatology was not caused by her husband wanting a divorce. The symptoms arose because she could not decide what course of action she should take to resolve the dilemma.

As soon as the woman was helped to see where the cause of the tension lay, Cohen terminated the session. He congratulated her again for the progress they had made and assured her that at their next session he would help her to sort everything out.

The two of us went for a coffee and Len Cohen said to me, 'Peter, when you have got as far as we have done today, the next step is to apply my "therapy of logical choices", and you do that by getting her to tell you what lines of action are open to *her*, which course *she* would prefer to take, and then explain to you why one choice is superior to any other. The third phase is to ask her why she hasn't followed through the choice she has told you would be the best for her, and that will lead you automatically to the fourth step, because you then have the logical choices defined. And the fourth step is to ask the $64,000 question, "Would you like me to help you so that you can do what you really want to?"

'If she agrees, then I go ahead, possibly using a hypnotic routine like your Reality Therapy suggestions. But if she says, "No", then you have to go through the entire process again, asking why she does not want your help. Or, you could tell her to go away, and make a new appointment when she does decide she wants your help.'

After my initiation into this new form of therapeutic procedure, Dr Cohen and I worked together for a little more than a year, and since we parted company, due to his taking up a new position overseas and prior to his appointment as a Professor of Psychology at an American university, I have found this combined methodology of logical choices plus hypnosis, to be the most effective and efficient treatment available to the psychotherapist. I am only amazed that more practitioners both here and in the United States, even if they do not use hypnosis, haven't become more aware of its tremendous potential. Fortunately there is a good chance that Len Cohen will be returning to England in the near future, on a working vacation, to teach his technique at the newly established Institute of Psychosomatic Therapy.

However, the most important statement Len made to me was, 'You will find that the cause of all functional neuroses and anxiety states is the inability of the people to make decisions. Peter, it is this inability to make decisions that is the bane of our civilization. Everyone wants someone else to make their decisions for them, because that frees them from a fear of personal failure. And, to make matters worse, our schools, both in Britain and the United States, actually teach our kids to be indecisive.'

This inability to make decisions is not confined to major issues. It occurs in minor matters like a wife asking her husband, 'Which would you rather have, tea or coffee?', or 'What dress shall I wear tonight?'

The buying of a dress or a car can give rise to apprehension, hence when the wife gets home she puts the dress on, and asks her husband, 'Do you like it, dear? There were a couple of dresses in the store that I liked, but I think this one suited me best. Don't you agree?' She is asking for confirmation to support her decision and to allay her anxiety.

The man who has bought a car begins to wonder if he should not have purchased another model because he had read somewhere that the other was allegedly superior. As he cannot tolerate his doubts he begins boasting about the capabilities of his new car, hoping that his friends will agree with the wisdom of his choice.

To trace the cause of this indecision, it is necessary to return to childhood, as most youngsters are rarely given an opportunity to make a decision. Their lives are regulated by the parents with, 'Do what you are told,' 'Go and put your coat on as you will not be warm enough,' 'It does not matter whether you are tired or not, it is bedtime, so off you go to bed,' plus a host of similar dictatorial commands. Just what the child thinks or feels is ignored, because mothers and fathers are sure that their age, and the fact they had sexual intercourse to produce an offspring, has endowed them with certain inalienable rights. Nor does this criticism imply that children should be allowed to run wild. Children themselves do not want that, and Dr Wilhelm Reich, the man considered to be the innovator of children's rights, was opposed to youngsters taking over and ruling the family roost.

His view was that children are human beings just like their parents, and both should be respected by each other. Exactly what he meant was classically illustrated by his wife, Ilse Ollendorf Reich, in the biography of her husband, *Wilhelm Reich*.[1]

When their son, Peter, started at nursery school he became enamoured with crayoning and colouring, and would use any wall of the house as a surface for his art work. Reich respected his son's desire to draw, but carefully explained to Peter that the house belonged to all of them, and as many people came to visit him, Reich's walls could not be used. However, Peter was assured he was completely free to draw upon the walls of his own room, and to facilitate the artistic endeavours of their son, the Reichs had Peter's bedroom walls painted with a washable paint,

[1] Elek Books Ltd., London, 1969.

and then gave him water colours and finger paints which he used enthusiastically.

Mrs Reich continued the story by relating how Peter invited his father and the famous British educationist A. S. Neill to visit his room and do some painting with him. Something they both thoroughly enjoyed. But the important aspect of this vignette was how Reich and his friend Neill waited to be invited into the boy's room instead of Reich automatically assuming, when he bought the paints, he had a *right* to show Peter, on Peter's walls, how to use them.

Some dear friends of mine also adopted the policy of allowing their son to make decisions for himself so that he could become self-regulatory, instead of being regulated, and it was a pleasure to see how their three-and-a-half-year-old boy was handed a menu when we were all dining in a restaurant, and then asked, seriously, what he would like to eat.

By the time he was four years old he was quite used to making his own decisions. He decided, among other things, what he would wear when he got up in the morning, what time he wanted to go to bed, and it surprised many visitors to his home to note that he went off to bed quietly whenever he was tired. And far from being the 'little monster' so graphically depicted by regulating disciplinarians, he was a well-adjusted, intelligent young man.

Most children do not have the advantage of the right parents, as the small boy I have mentioned above. They have to learn self-denial and how *not* to make decisions as they try to win the love of their parents by doing what is expected of them.

And as Dr Cohen said, our educational systems have to accept an equal share of the responsibility for perpetuating indecisiveness.

The schools have failed to recognize the needs of their pupils, and instead of fulfilling the task of educating the young people confined within their establishments, for the word 'educate' means to rear a complete person, the authorities have concentrated upon developing the cognitive, or mental processes, to the detriment of all the other human attributes which are equally necessary for the adult to cope with life.

The vast majority of educationists have ignored the facts staring them in the face, that the children entering school have not only been made insecure by their upbringing, but have already started to use certain defence mechanisms which could lead to future maladjustment and neuroses. One headmaster told me when I tried to discuss this with him, 'I think there is too much psychology in education today. We are here to teach.' He did not want to acknowledge that schools are for children, and are not edifices built to enable academics to show how clever they are by producing a small percentage of pupils able to get good examination results.

Due to the need to win constant approval, schools everywhere are well populated with over-achieving pupils who, when set a task, have to do it better than anyone else in the class to gain teacher approval. Year after year they come near the top of the class, but if something happens and they cannot maintain their position, they collapse like the young man mentioned in an earlier chapter who only got high examination results in nine subjects instead of the ten he felt necessary to get recognition.

If these boys and girls are still at school when they meet failure, and they do not manifest mental or physical distress, they have a strong tendency to become the rebels or bullies, because that gives them another type of approval.

Despite these dangers to the pupils, the idolization of the over-achievers, together with undue importance placed upon academic achievement, is still very much a part of the system.

At a British public school of some repute there is a large notice board on public display with the names of all the students of the lower school on it. Each week the scholastic attainments of each boy are marked alongside his name, together with his position in the class. Obviously this version of the public pillory is meant to give recognition to those who 'have worked hard', and to inspire the remainder to become competitive, and strive even harder to receive public acclaim.

For those who are at the top of their class the board does give a boost to the false self-image the youngsters have been forced into acquiring, but it also creates unnecessary tension among the members of the elitist group who have continually to exert themselves to maintain their exalted position.

The board fulfils another function which is ignored. It reinforces failure in the less academically capable who, although they have tried hard to improve their position in the class, never quite make the grade. They soon learn their chances of rectifying the status quo are nil, and give up trying.

It would be pleasant if I could write that the public school was exceptional, but it is not. Most schools send out end of term reports giving a subject by subject grading, and these have exactly the same effect as the display board. If anything they are even more damaging, because some parents who find their children are not among the school elite resort to emotional blackmail.

To entice their child into doing better promises are made with specific conditions attached to them: 'If you are in the top three of your class by the end of next term we will buy you the bike that you want.' And to gain the parents' love, for that is what the bike represents in the child's mind, the boy or girl is submitted to stress, and if, despite all their efforts, they cannot attain the parental objective, and there is no new bike waiting for them, this is the equivalent of the withdrawal of parental love.

Some years ago there was a popular song, 'An Apple for the Teacher', and although it is no longer common practice for pupils to try and win the teacher's approval by such simple bribery, every class in every school, in every country, has those young people who are so insecure that their behaviour qualifies them as teacher's pets.

The rationale behind this manoeuvre is that the pupils have already learned at home never to attempt any task which they might fail to complete, as that could bring reproach down upon them, and it is safer to try and win approval by always being ready to give up playtime to help the mother or father. In the classroom the children, to use their peers' description, are 'right creeps', and always ready to run messages, stay in at playtime to tidy up the classroom, or to stay after school to clean the blackboard.

This servile behaviour pleases some teachers, it boosts their ego, and when the end of term report is compiled the reward appears in the comment, 'Has a very pleasing personality, although could do better in some subjects.'

But what happens when this currying of favour goes unrecognized? One boy whom I will refer to as James came from a broken home. His father had left when James was still young, yet he had an idolized image of him, and saw in every male teacher in his school a father-substitute. James tried to please the men around him in every way that he could in order to obtain from them the regard he had never known from his own father. The teachers did not understand his behaviour. They were repelled by his obsequiousness, and began to regularly punish him for lack of work.

Before long James was relegated to a remedial class as an educationally backward boy, and to make matters worse for him the new teacher was a woman, someone he had no rapport with, and no reason to work for.

The case of James came to light when Mr David McGlown, B.Ed, was researching into 'Emotional Factors in Apparent Backwardness'[2] in Lancashire schools. The McGlown document showed that many children are labelled as educationally backward, whereas in reality they were emotionally disadvantaged.

A young girl Mr McGlown worked with produced very little school work, hence her being in a remedial section, and he discovered she was intelligent but had a weak self-image. She could not, and would not, complete the set lessons because she was sure they would show the teachers what a bad person she was. Her dilemma was poignantly expressed when she was asked to draw, separately, two pictures, one of a 'good person' and the other of a 'bad person'.

The remarkable thing about her drawings was that the bad person she drew was a self-portrait, complete with hands and feet, while her pictorial concept of a good person was the opposite of her in every way, and had no hands or feet.

By itself the omission of the hands and feet from one of the drawings would mean nothing, but as McGlown spent a lot of time with other information-producing procedures he was able to arrive at a confirmed interpretation; the good girl had no feet because they would not walk her into trouble, and had no hands as they would not do anything others could call bad.

[2] An unpublished thesis dated October 1970.

However, most children's insecurity is not so easily recognizable. There are many who do exactly what they are told, but no more and no less. They present no overt problems to their teachers and therefore are not seen as children with a problem. Yet it is there. The barrier which prevents them from ever achieving their full academic potential is the fear of incurring displeasure by exposing themselves to individual scrutiny. They prefer to remain buried within the security of the mass of mediocrity.

I could continue providing different personality profiles to illustrate how education caters for the bright student, the future leaders, and teaches the mass of pupils to be unthinking adults, but this would not prove anything. The opponents of whole-people education would attack by saying I was only quoting the exceptional child and miss the point I am trying to make, that the educational system is geared to mass-production. That it fails to teach each child how to think for itself, to make personal decisions, and accordingly the teaching methods currently employed have turned our schools into breeding grounds for future victims of the stress plague.

These are serious accusations, and need elaboration. A lot of publicity has been given to the changes being made in the curriculum, and in the infant-elementary schools this is particularly noticeable. The children no longer sit in rows of desks, copying down meaningless symbols from a blackboard. They are encouraged to learn through personal experience. A step in the right direction. But only a step, because as the pupils proceed up through the educational pyramid, knowledge is forced into them in the form of facts and data which they are meant to remember and regurgitate like a mini-computer when the examinations are held.

As future members of a competitive society the examinees are aware that the future can depend upon the marks they receive. This is totally unfair.

An examination does not assess how much the student knows. At best it tells the examiners how good the memory is, and even as a memory test it is suspect due to the anxiety factor. For if the anxiety level is high, memory recall is impaired. Stupid mistakes are made as the candidate tries to force himself to do well and some will suffer an examination amnesia, where the mind goes blank until the test is over. The girls have an added disadvantage. If they are about to menstruate, or are having a menstrual period, this can affect their performance, and the outcome.

When these facts have been presented by progressive educationists the official reaction is to admit that the exam system of assessment is imperfect, but does help to isolate the brighter pupils from the mass. A nice way of saying 'some have to fall by the wayside'!

As long as the attitude prevails that higher education is the prerogative of future leaders – the *Führer* principle of Nazi Germany carefully hidden behind a smokescreen of democratic jargon – then the competitive marking system and the ensuing examinations must remain sacrosanct. Only when it is decided to educate the whole person, helping everyone to be self-regulative instead of regulated, then teachers will begin marking, if they haven't scrapped the idea altogether, each student's work against his own past performance, thereby encouraging personal advancement and building confidence without stress. The children will be taught how to solve problems for themselves instead of being told 'this is the correct way to do it', and discussions will, whenever possible, be the source of information and knowledge instead of the teacher and text-books acting as fountains of infallible wisdom.

In the studies completed on teenage scholars, and their criticisms of the education they receive, the main bone of contention is the lack of verbal communication between the staff and themselves, plus their lack of recognition as individuals, things which will not be remedied, at least in Britain, by the construction of mammoth comprehensive schools where a thousand or more children will be herded together to become more rebellious at the further loss of identity.

Upon emerging from our present seats of learning (other than the universities), the post-school citizen has either learned to accept the position society has designated for him, and is content to stay hidden in the security of the mass; or has the desire to break away from the social structure which has tried to mould him into a non-person, and to seek his security among the adherents of the alternative society. Really it does not matter which group he elects to join, as he finds himself in the same trap. Deep within himself he has the yearning to be free, to know the freedom of self-expression he has been denied since he was born. But he needs to belong to a group, and needs a leader to tell him what to do.

What the group stands for is immaterial. The hippies who want to dismantle the capitalist system and replace it by collectivism, with the rights of the individual being respected, wear their uniforms, and look for their *Führer*, even if he is an Eastern mystic or a Western drug-escapist. And the *Führer* needs the group to give him the courage to lead.

Little wonder that John Aitkinhead, one of Britain's leading advocates of self-regulatory education told a group of student-teachers in 1972, 'Our schools are breeding grounds for fascists.'

Chapter 6
The sexual signal

'Whenever I am upset I don't want to have sexual intercourse. I either forget all about it, or prefer to masturbate', a young married man told me during one of his visits.

Neither was his comment unusual, as it is recognized by medical practitioners that when stress reaches a certain level both men and women lose interest in sexual intercourse, and this has led many doctors to see the decline of sexual interest and activity as a signal of the patient's distressed condition.

However, this observation may be putting the cart before the horse. It was the late Dr Wilhelm Reich who found while he was working with Sigmund Freud that the patients who did not respond to psychoanalysis had one thing in common, an unsatisfactory sex life, and he postulated in his book, *Die Funktion des Orgasmus*,[1] that a complete sexual functioning was essential to good physical and mental health.

His definition of complete sexual functioning was the ability to surrender conscious control at the moment of orgasm, and allow the body to enter into a spontaneous, convulsive spasm. This full orgasmic response was described to me as, 'It was marvellous. I didn't know what I was doing, but there was a tremendous sense of freedom, just as if I were up in the clouds.' And according to Reich, the true orgasm permits the discharge of energy from the body. If it is not released in this way he concluded the energy would accumulate, and the total organism would ultimately be in a state of tension, leading to either mental disorders in the form of neuroses or phobias, or physical disabilities, both due to the body being kept rigid rather than relaxed.

[1] International Psychoanalytischer Verlag, Vienna, 1927. Also published in English as *The Function of the Orgasm*, Panther Books, St Albans, 1968.

When Wilhelm Reich formulated and published his views he was ridiculed and attacked. The reason for the vitriolic reaction was, and still is, that what he wrote and lectured about affronted the millions of people who are non-orgasmic. It was an attack upon those who had been taught by their religious leaders and parents that sexual intercourse is only for procreation and does not need to be pleasurable, and it was an anathema to people who had been conditioned by society into accepting that sex plays a very minor part in life.

Confirmation of Reich's emphasizing the importance of releasing the internal energy through orgasmic convulsions comes, surprisingly, from the ranks of his bitterest critics, orthodox psychiatry. For when chemotherapy – drugs – have failed to ameliorate stress disorders, psychiatrists frequently turn to electro *convulsive* therapy (ECT). The treatment is often successful if it is followed up with individual or group therapy to assist the patient to cope with the environmental setting which produced the stress. But if there is no follow-up, other than drugs, the chances are that ECT will only provide temporary relief, and the patient has to return for a further series of artificially induced convulsions.

This type of therapy is not as new as psychiatry would have the lay population believe. Throughout history the medicine man, be he witch-doctor, voodoo priest, or the modern, highly trained medical practitioner, has instinctively known the therapeutic value of convulsions.

In Africa and those parts of the West Indies where voodoo still flourishes, the medicine man will induce an altered state of awareness in his patients, perhaps by the repetitive rhythm of a drum beat, which reaches its climax when the bodies of the men and women are racked by uncontrollable and violent tremors.

Dr Franz Anton Mesmer, mistakenly attributed to be the father of medical hypnosis, produced convulsions in his patients as a result of their treatment with animal magnetism, and some of Professor Sigmund Freud's own successes could be explained in the same way, because a proportion of his patients underwent a rapid recovery when they were regressed back to an earlier, traumatic episode in their life, and released the hitherto pent-up emotion while abreacting.

The psychiatrist fails to see the historic connection with what he is doing by putting an electric shock across the temporal lobes of the brain, and while he cannot explain why and how ECT works, he continues to reject the Reichian concept, although every man and woman who has experienced the release of total orgasm could tell him how wonderful is the feeling of well-being that follows.

The psychiatrists should talk to epileptics about how they feel after they have had a series of convulsions that comprise the epileptic spasm. A lady told me, 'it is a sensation of being free. A feeling I can do things that I could not do before.' And a Swiss psychologist, Dr A. Leder from Zurich, supported this premise in a report he wrote on adult epileptics.

Dr Leder urged doctors to get their epileptic patients to talk about the frustrations which act as a trigger for their attacks, and he said these may be sexual in origin, a way of escaping from a position they find intolerable, or an outlet for unexpressable aggression. In his, Leder's, opinion early psychotherapy assists patients to cope with their problem with a minimum of medication, and with less spasms.[a]

Mary, a young, unmarried woman in therapy, had a history of migraine, and the seizures occurred as often as three or four times a week, when she was physically sick and was forced to go into a darkened room to sleep.

While undergoing analysis she told her therapist how, as a little girl, her parents had made her feel she must always do what they told her, and gave her the impression she would lose their love and positive regard if she failed them.

Her personality mirrored her upbringing. She was a meticulous person who felt she must always have prior knowledge of what was going to happen, and get various opinions as to how she should act. Then she would mentally rehearse her reactions to ensure nothing unexpected could confront her. This mental rigidity was expressed in the way she held her body and in her

[a] See the British medical weekly newspaper, *Pulse*, 15 January 1969. Item reference C/058.

inability to relax, because of the permanent fear that if she let her guard slip for a single second she would commit a compulsive act which later she would have cause to regret.

Mary had a strong desire to be liked and loved by everyone, hence her need to be on guard at all times to prevent her from giving offence.

Sexually she was equally compulsive. If a man wanted to have sexual intercourse with her, and she felt she wanted the man to like her, she would consent even though she was not sexually attracted to him. But the only position she enjoyed the sexual act was for her to be on top of the man. That allowed her to keep her own orgasmic, bodily feelings under control.

When asked why it was necessary to regulate her response, which was a natural one, Mary answered, 'I dare not let go, I would be overwhelmed.'

On the occasions when a man she did not like, who was repulsive to her, made sexual advances, she had the powerful feeling she had to agree to them so as not to incur his hostility. But on the other hand, the thought of having intercourse with him was nauseating. Finding herself in a double-bind, and not knowing how to act or how to escape, Mary's pulse in the neck would begin to throb, and 'I would feel it building up inside me until it reached my eyes and forehead, then it would spill over, going down to my stomach, after which I would be as sick as a pig. Once I had been sick and allowed to sleep, when I woke up I would be better.'

Asked what it was that built up inside her, Mary answered, 'Pressure. It is difficult to describe, but it is as if my heart was beating too strongly, forcing the blood up into my head.'

With the passage of time Mary found herself in an increasing number of situations where she did not know how to act, and her migraine, her own particular defence mechanism, became increasingly activated.

As she began to understand the part her parents had unwittingly played in her intense desire to be liked, she began to maturate mentally, but she still had periodic migraine attacks.

These persisted until the day she telephoned her therapist. 'I thought I had better tell you that I masturbated for the first time in my life last night, and I had a good night's sleep, and feel great.'

The therapist had not recommended masturbation as part of the therapy. They had simply discussed together the possible reasons underlying her sexual compulsiveness, and lack of orgasmic response.

Mary discovered for herself, as a result of being a more relaxed and confident woman, whenever she felt tension building up inside her, if she masturbated it restored relaxation, and the long-term migraine pattern disappeared.

Another married woman in her early thirties had a long history of so-called nervous disorders, including depression, and obses-sive-compulsive neurosis – the need to fulfil a ritualistic proce-dure to ensure a feeling of safety – which in her case was a fetish about cleanliness; a fear of poisonous germs, making her clean everything in the house over and over. As I was following up the line of thought being presented in this chapter, I enquired about her sex life, and it was non-existent. That in itself I recognized proved nothing as her anxiety could have been responsible.

Slowly the aetiology came to the surface. What triggered off her bouts of obsessive-compulsion and depression was a feeling that she could not continue to maintain a clean and tidy home, something her parents had insisted upon during her early, forma-tive years, and if she let the house become untidy it would prove what they had repeatedly told her as a child, that she was a 'slut'.

I asked her what the word 'slut' meant to her.

She didn't want to answer, but I kept silent until she replied. 'Well, it is a woman who thinks about nothing else but having sex with any man that happens to be around.'

This provided me with a natural lead into talking about her own sexuality which she had admitted had never been as good as she knew it could and should be.

'I have never been able to accept the idea that I like sex,' she told me.

'Why do you think you are unable to accept the idea that you like sex?' I countered in true Len Cohen fashion.

'It goes back to my parents, I suppose. When I was in my teens they kept on harping about keeping myself "pure" and "clean", and that sex was "dirty".'

'And what do those words "pure" and "clean" mean to you?'

Her voice filled with anger. 'They mean I had to stay pure and clean. I had to keep everything, including me, pure and clean to please my bloody mother, and be like her. God! She was always cleaning, and she made me be like her. But I am not like her,' she sobbed, 'I am me. I want to be me, but I can't. I can't let her down.'

The breakthrough in therapy came later when she was able to face the fact that her real fear was of letting herself enjoy sexual intercourse, as that would confirm she was a slut.

As the insight into her problems became clear, she saw that she needed to obsessively clean the house to prove she was clean, and in order to tire herself out physically to avoid having sex with her husband. The germs she was frightened of were symbolic. They would punish her if she ever permitted herself the pleasure she knew would come through the sexual embrace and a complete orgasm.

These and similar female sexual problems rarely come to light, because the way a woman is built permits her to lie back during intercourse, and put on an act of enjoyment, taking deep breaths at the right moment, simulating orgasm.

They pretend for a variety of reasons. A number of women are sexual 'givers', like the patient Mary with migraine, and if anything they are to be pitied, because they reach a time when giving no longer fulfils their need, then sexual advances have to be resisted. Other women act to make their husbands feel they are *men*, and can satisfy any woman, any time. Yet as far as the majority are concerned, they have to pretend so that they can continue deluding themselves that they are real, orgasmic women.

Nor is the lack of orgasmic response confined to females. As most men are able to obtain an erection and have intercourse through to ejaculation, they assume that ejaculation is the same thing as an orgasm. They are wrong, because the great proportion of men are only sexual performers. When they have intercourse they are acting. They remain in control of themselves throughout to ensure they satisfy their partners, and their pleasure is derived from the partner thinking they are magnificent lovers.

And at this point I can imagine the screams of protest and downright anger being hurled in my direction by members of my own sex who are insulted by my criticism of their sexual prowess. I know the arguments they offer in their defence, as I have heard them often enough. 'I enjoy my sex,' is one indignant answer;

'I do release tension during intercourse, and feel better afterwards, therefore I am orgasmically potent.'

Then there is the final abuse when all arguments fail, 'You are some sort of nut with sex on the brain. You should have it down there where I have got it.'

Yet, let these fine upstanding men – and no pun is intended! – listen to the comments of their female partners: 'He makes me feel I am being used';

'There is no loving in his sex, all he wants to do is get on with it';

'He thinks I should be ready to enjoy it, because he is ready and randy';

'From the moment he puts his hand on my breast I know exactly what he is going to do to try and arouse me. What he doesn't know is that he always does the same thing, and how boring it is';

'Most of the time he goes on and on like some bloody machine, urging me to climax all the time. He won't stop until I have pretended I have had an orgasm.'

Here is a question for both men and women: 'How often have you ladies heard, and you men said towards the end of sexual intercourse, "Have you *come*, dear?"?'

There is no need for you to write to me giving me your answer. I am already aware that millions of you have heard it, and said it. So, now let me tell you what the question means. The man who asks it is a performer asking for applause. It is simply another way of saying, 'I did well, didn't I dear? So praise me, give me the warranted applause.' He is a little boy asking his mother to pay him a compliment to show that he is 'a good boy' and is loved!

Men and women find it difficult to admit their lack of true orgasm, and this makes them attack anyone who spotlights their deficiency. It is why Sigmund Freud was attacked and reviled for expounding his theory of infantile sexuality, and the reason Wilhelm Reich was slandered, libelled, misrepresented, and his documented findings showing the causative link between the lack of total orgasm and psychosomatic illness studiously ignored. People do not want to be reminded of their lost, or never discovered, sexual pleasure as it makes them feel inadequate.

It was Freud who saw the origins of anxiety and neurosis in the Oedipal conflict, where infantile sexuality leads us to fall sexually in love with the parent of the opposite sex, and see the parent of the same sex as a rival. And every psychotherapist has seen patients whose troubles seem to stem from the Oedipal situation. But there could be another explanation for this conflict.

As the male child matures physically and mentally he realizes that his chances of getting the desired tender loving contact with his mother are diminishing, and between the ages of four and seven years he makes his last attempt to obtain it. Quite unconsciously he studies his relationship with his mother, and is forced into the conclusion that his father is getting all the physical contact he should have. He sees them sleeping together, going out together, and naturally he is jealous. Not because he wants to make love to his mother but to get the contact he has been denied since birth. And I have to add, that since all physical contact has some pleasurable, sexual connotation, the child may find the contact he gets arouses him sexually.

For a time the boy does treat his father as a rival in his fight for contact. When he does not succeed he rejects his mother, and tries to get it instead from his father. As the father rarely provides what he wants he is forced to reject him as well, and tries to accept that he will never get what he has missed.

It is to protect himself from his own inner sense of loss that the boy enters what Freud termed the latency period, a time when he is not too interested in sex and trying to obtain contact, and he manages to keep this defence intact until he reaches puberty. With the advent of ejaculation and sexual manhood the boy turns to masturbation as he is unable to trust girls: his mother was a girl and she rejected him.

The effects in later life upon men and women, for women go

through the same phase, of their struggle between the ages of four and seven years can be serious.

A married man with children had a fear he had never been able to disclose, and it prevented him from relaxing. He was frightened he was a homosexual, because he was attracted to older men and tried to touch them whenever he had the opportunity. This compulsion scared him, hence his being always on guard to stop himself from getting older men to make love to him.

During the therapeutic sessions it transpired that as a child he became emotionally alienated from his mother, and tried to establish communication with his father. Unfortunately for him, his father was unable to communicate effectively with anyone, and covered up his personality deficiency by masquerading as a military martinet who gave orders or made plain his views. Once the patient saw he had been trying to find a substitute father throughout the years, his fear of being a homosexual disappeared.

But had one of the older men he had been attracted to been another homosexual, the chances are that he would have taken advantage of the patient's tentative approaches, and anal intercourse could have taken place, with the result that the patient may well have become a practising homosexual. He would have misinterpreted the physical contact of anal intercourse as the love he had earlier wanted from his father.

Most practising homosexuals are the 'arrogant aristocrats of the deviants', and do not want to accept the concept that their sexual behaviour comes from a disturbed childhood. They prefer to see themselves as being the 'third sex' and 'gay', but as Dr Alexander Lowen, MD, the New York psychiatrist and head of the Institute of Bio-Energetics, said in 1963 during a series of lectures on sex and personality, 'But if the homosexual is gay, he is certainly neither happy nor joyful. Under analysis he proves to be one of the most tragic figures of our times.'[3]

From the case history of the man who thought he was homosexual, plus Dr Lowen's comment, two important issues arise: firstly, it explains why young men feel a strong antagonism when they are in the presence of a homosexual, because they too have

[3] *Sex and Personality: A Study in Orgiastic Potency.* The Institute of Bio-Energetics, New York, 1963, page 11.

known the same paternal deprivation and have the same deep repressed desire to try and recapture it, but dare not as it could lead them into being 'one of those queers'.

Secondly, if the hypothesis I have presented is correct, does it mean that homosexuals can be helped to become hetero-sexual?

Rather than give my own views on this, I prefer to relate what happened in London on 18 May 1972, when Dr Arthur Janov was giving a lecture on his primal scream therapy.

At question time a man asked Dr Janov if he stood by a statement he made in his book *The Primal Scream*, that homosexuality was a neurotic condition. Janov answered with a blunt 'Yes'. At which point the questioner lost control of himself and became verbally aggressive.

To counter the tirade launched against him, Janov told the audience how he arrived at such a conclusion. At his Institute in Los Angeles, California, many male homosexuals had been accepted as patients, not to be treated for their sexual problem, but for other reasons, and Janov found that as they released all the pain caused by primal separation anxiety, they emerged as hetero-sexuals.

Still unsatisfied with 'gay boys' being referred to as neurotics, the questioner dared Dr Janov to explain how some homosexuals were born with an additional female chromosome, and were therefore biologically homosexuals instead of neurotics subverted by their infant environment.

Janov's reply was to the effect that the womb was still a human environment, and it was possible that the mother's mental and physical state in pregnancy could cause the chromosome imbalance, and, accordingly, homosexuality must still be a neuroticism.

Yet with putting into print Janov's answer, tentatively confirmed by the rat-research undertaken by Dr Ingeborg Ward, there is a danger which I encountered when a father brought his effeminate son to see me, and demanded, 'Mr Blythe, I want you to use hypnosis to make this queer into a real man.'

What the father overlooked was that his own overbearing manner could have been the reason for his son's being homosexual, and he did not take into consideration whether his son wanted to be a hetero-sexual male. As it turned out the young man didn't, and as no one has the moral right to try and dictate what life-style another should adopt, I refused to comply with the father's wishes.

The female reaction to the Oedipal conflict has the same effects. A young woman had strong lesbian tendencies, and although she was very feminine in her looks, build and dress, anything but the butch-type portrayed in salacious magazines, she always saw herself in the dominant male sexual role.

She had wanted her mother to pay more attention to her than to her father, but her manoeuvres in that direction met with failure and she unconsciously made the decision that the only way she could get her mother to notice her was by attempting to be masculine. And this mother-fixation was apparent when anyone saw the type of women the patient was attracted to, because they were not frilly, girlish girls, they all had the mature figures of womanhood.

The girls who are arrested at the stage of development when they are trying to get contact from their fathers will attach themselves to older men. This usually results in their having a temporary, sexual affair with the older man, and that is sufficient to free them from their emotional impediment. Others marry the older man, and while some of these spring-and-autumn marriages are successful, they are prone to failure because the time can come when the girl no longer requires the child-father contact, and is ready to enter into a full sexual relationship.

Another case taken from among many shows why I have placed this new interpretation of Freud's Oedipal conflict, because it shows that the neurotic behaviour begins before the ages of four to seven years.

To start at the beginning will help the reader to see how complicated unravelling a human dilemma can be. A young man, Robin, married and was happy knowing he had someone who loved him for what he was, and someone he could love and trust in return.

For a time the relationship was idyllic, but his wife was far from sure she was ready to accept the role of a housewife. She did not know if she would continue loving her husband, because in the past she had experienced falling out of love after a couple of months. Her uncertainty made it difficult for her to respond and communicate openly and honestly. The husband did not notice the reticence and was busy making plans for their future.

The crunch came when a former male friend of Janet's arrived to spend a few days with them, and the wife appeared to spend more time with her friend than her husband. Robin saw this as an estrangement, becoming unsure of himself, and did not know how to act with her. He lost interest in sexual intercourse, and when they did he was unable to let go of himself and ejaculate. Later he told me he felt Janet had betrayed him.

When her husband retreated inside his bodily armour, Janet discovered she really did need him, and her love for Robin was the real thing, and would last. But the more she tried to recapture his affection the more introverted he became, making Janet feel she did not know what to do to restore their former loving status.

That is where I entered upon their scene. Robin was unable to relax, had a high level of inner tension, could not have the physical contact he wanted with his wife, and felt he had a divided personality; wanting one thing, but doing the exact opposite. He also said that when he felt in a good mood he would dress up in his wife's clothes, and that worried him a little.

He complained of never having a meaningful relationship with his father, irrespective of how hard he tried, and the same with his mother. 'She never listens to what I am saying,' he told me. 'It was the same when I was a child. She would ask me a question, but when I tried to answer it, really communicate with her, she didn't listen. She's never listened to me. I remember being aware of this when I was about two-and-a-half years old, so I used to go upstairs, get dressed in my sister's clothes, and come down and give a mannequin parade. She used to notice me then, and she would sit and watch me, talk to me, for ages.'

It transpired his mother had wanted a little girl when she was pregnant, and had already chosen a name for her. Now I had the key to his problem. Robin had the idea firmly implanted in his unconscious mind that if he had been a little girl he would have got all the attention he wanted, and he saw confirmation of it when he dressed up as a girl.

There was the foundation for his latent transvestism. Whenever he felt unloved he had the impulse to dress up in Janet's clothes so that she would, like his mother, give him signals that he was loved.

Yet, while he was dressing up in female apparel he knew, even if he could not admit it consciously, it was not the usual behaviour of an adult male, and he doubted his masculinity – the reason for his 'divided personality'.

As only a few people receive extreme conditioning like Robin, Wilhelm Reich wanted to understand what happened to the mass to make them non-orgasmic, and he began to see that the seeds of sexual impotency were actually sown by the parents.

Any normal child growing up soon discovers that the genital area is a source of pleasure. A fact recognized by mothers who masturbate their infant, boy child when he shows signs of bad temper.

In the infant the sexual exploration is tolerated to a degree, but as the child gets older the usual parental reaction is to stop it by pulling the hand away, and saying, 'Don't do that, dear. It is not nice'. If it persists the verbal deterrent, 'Nice girls don't do that', is reinforced by a smack, and threats are made. 'A blackbird will come down and peck it off, Jimmy', or 'If you keep on doing that it will drop off', and the poor boy has to walk around all day with a sticking-plaster in his pocket ready to stick it back on again.

With the passing years children invent games to mask their sexual inquisitiveness. They play 'Mummies and Daddies' or 'Doctors and Nurses' when no adults are around, and by the time they are indulging in this game-playing they are already sexually inhibited, because they have to create fantasies to make sex acceptable.

Of course we adults know our children play these games, but if we catch them at it then we over-react and resort to the form of punishment we have found to be the most effective.

To overcome this repressive parental posturing Reich advocated that children be allowed to enjoy their sexuality, and while he was still living in Vienna, in the late 1920s, he proposed that 'love houses' be made available to the young to enable them to have sexual intercourse in congenial surroundings, instead of furtively sneaking their sexual encounters in parks, standing in dark, draughty doorways, in the constant fear of being caught. Only when this happened, Reich maintained, would they grow up free from orgasmic limitations.

In support of his proposals Reich quoted the findings of the anthropologist Bronislaw B. Malinowski who had studied the sexual life of the Trobriand Islanders in Melanesia.

Malinowski's book *The Sexual Life of Savages*[4] recorded seeing the island children being encouraged to experiment sexually as often as they wished, and with whom they chose, and instead of growing up into irresponsible sexual athletes, they married and had happy stable relationships.

It does not require a vivid imagination to envisage the hostility Reich engendered by his ideas, because even in our present, so-called, permissive society, if a psychiatrist were to publicize the same views he would be ostracized and most likely committed to a mental hospital as a corrupter of youthful innocence.

But I doubt if Reich's ideas had been put into operation they would have had the impact he wanted. By the time the Viennese children of the 1920s, and the children of today, reach adolescence they are already crippled and cowed. The needs for phantasy, created by the taboos imposed in infancy, were and are so deeply engrained they require help plus experience to overcome them.

My years as a hypno-analyst and psychotherapist have taught me that adults, too, need their phantasies to make sex acceptable.

The widespread female phantasy of wanting to be raped is typical. When wives urge their husbands in the middle of intercourse to 'Rape me. Rape me. Harder ... Harder ... Let go ... Do whatever you want with me', it is not an expression of their enjoyment. It is a plea. They really do want to be raped.

Certain women are unable to vocalize their desire, thinking their husbands would be shocked, and they frequently imagine they are tied to the four corners of the bed, powerless to move or protest throughout.

Another ploy is in keeping with the Victorian adage that a man wants his wife to be a lady in the drawing-room and in the lounge,

[4]Routledge & Kegan Paul Ltd., London, 1932, 1969.

but a whore in bed. Charming, sedate women find they can only liberate their sexuality when they, and their husbands, cast aside all the trappings of polite society, and lapse into the use of four-letter Anglo-Saxon words to describe their anatomies, what they are doing to each other, and what they want their partner to do.

Behind both excursions into phantasy there lies the same explanation. By using an unusual form of language expression the woman can pretend she is not really involved in what is happening. It must be someone else, someone whose speech shows that they are on a lower, more animalistic plane than she is.

By feigning being raped she is not responsible for what is happening, and if she responds it is not because she would normally act in such an abandoned manner, it is the situation forced upon her.

A married lady who had been criminally raped by an intruder fought the man off as long as she could, and finally surrendered to the inevitable. Until then she had been non-orgasmic, but to her horror she found herself spontaneously responding to the rapist's uninhibited, strong body movements. She listened to herself moaning and screaming with unadulterated pleasure as she had one orgasm after another. After the attacker had left she reported the incident to the police, but long after the criminal proceedings had ended she had a giant sized guilt-complex due to involuntary response. She sought treatment, and was helped before her feelings got out of hand.

Another woman who had been married a number of times was less fortunate. Her complaint was compulsive, sexual promiscuity which had wrecked two of her marriages. No man had ever satisfied her and it would have been easy to diagnose her condition as nymphomania. But she did not want to seduce all the men she came into contact with. Her one aim was to live happily with the right man.

While she consciously related her life story to her therapist she mentioned being criminally raped as a fourteen-year-old. Asked what effect it had had upon her, she spoke lucidly about the brutal details of the assault and the nightmares she had for years afterwards.

As the therapy progressed the memories she had isolated in her unconscious mind came back into consciousness. She cried out in protest, 'But I liked it. My whole body thrilled as I reached a climax, and I have never felt that way since. I want to feel that again, and there must be a man, somewhere, who can make me come alive as he did.'

That woman had spent the best years of her life searching for a man to rape her so that she could have an orgasm again without being held responsible for it!

Although it is not classified as a true phantasy, there is an anti-sex defence mechanism that is widely used by women. It is called the 'act of limitation' and it also has its origins in the way the parents, especially the mother, have brought them up to regard sex.

In this instance it refers to the millions of women who refuse to have sexual intercourse during the day or with the electric light on, and to those who cannot permit the act unless they continue to wear an item of clothing.

And their behaviour means that as long as they cannot see what is taking place, as long as their husband cannot see them naked, they are not committing an act which would, if their mother knew about it, result in them losing love.

Just how widespread this defence is became clear when the well known Irish comedian Dave Allen, told a joke during one of his shows on BBC television. Talking about the differences that exist between sexual expression in Britain and Ireland, he said the best contraceptive was 'to switch the light on!'

His audience of men and women laughed as they recognized the truth in his humour, but had Mr Allen explained to the ladies present what their refusal to have the light on meant, there would have been a storm of protest because the truth would have been too painful to tolerate.

The men laughed loudly at the feminine foible, but they had no reason to laugh too loudly, because many men become impotent when asked to perform naked, and with the light on, and they also use another act of limitation.

There are millions of men throughout the world who continue to use the sheath-contraceptive, the condom. I admit some of the popularity stems from availability, and they are a boon to the single man who meets a girl that is prepared to have intercourse. They also have the added attraction of giving some protection against venereal disease. It must also be admitted that some women are wary of taking the oral contraceptive, and the sheath is an alternative.

But, in spite of these legitimate motives many men prefer to use them, and a good percentage of them are unconsciously carrying out an act of limitation. As long as there is a barrier, irrespective of how thin and membranous it may be, between the sexual organs, they are not risking Mummy's and Daddy's righteous wrath.[5]

Here the women readers may ask, 'What are the common male phantasies?' They are many and varied, but a good proportion of men imagine that during the sexual act their partner is having sexual intercourse with another man, or alternatively, they are having sexual relations with another woman, perhaps someone they saw during the day.

In the same way that a woman's imagining being raped or made love to by another man makes sex acceptable and enjoyable for her, so do the two male phantasies I have mentioned. But neither the male or female can escape from the real reason why they are necessary. And for the man who conjures up a mental picture of another man having intercourse with his wife, he is unconsciously expressing doubts about his own sexual capability. This is evident after talking to those men who have translated their phantasy into reality and indulged in troilism – three people sharing a sexual experience simultaneously, but in this case two men and a woman.

They describe how they watch the other man having intercourse with their wife first, and the arousal effect the voyeurism has on them. Then when it is over and it is their turn, they have a sense of sexual freedom and abandon that is otherwise missing.

Few of them appreciate that their liberation is only possible because they have seen that their wife has been sexually satisfied

[5] By referring to the unconscious motivation for using a sheath contraceptive this does not imply, in any way, their lack of reliability, nor does it impugn the well-adjusted male who prefers to use them as an alternative contraceptive device.

by her earlier partner, and therefore they do not have to try and give a performance; they can simply enjoy themselves as they want to.

There is another explanation for the man being aroused by the idea of his wife actually having sexual intercourse with another man, and in the interest of accuracy I have to include it.

If a man feels his wife has a need for additional, extra-marital experience – and this can be for any number of reasons – instead of remaining in a state of permanent apprehension, wondering when it is going to happen and with whom, he can precipitate the deed, and as it takes place with his full knowledge it obviates the danger of his wife having to be furtive and lying to him.

However even this explanation may be a rationalization to cover up the man's insecurity. 'I may not be adequate, but I can make sure she continues to live with me, by making certain she is sexually satisfied by another.'

A warning, however, to the foolhardy. Experimenting with troilism can be fraught with danger, as many people have found to their cost. They thought they were devotees of the permissive society and felt it would put spice into a dull marriage, but one or other has found out later they could not accept their marital partner because he or she had practised it with someone else, and they had to separate.

Returning to the male phantasies. When a man imagines he is having sexual intercourse with another woman he is free to phantasize all the sexual antics he would like to try if only his wife were not his drawing-room lady.

If he asked his wife to do all the things he could ask a casual stranger he had picked up and bedded for the night to do, his wife might decide he was not the nice boy he had pretended to be – and the forms of his phantasies show he is not really nice at all in parental terms – and if she reached that conclusion she might leave him.

This is why married people having an extra-marital relationship find there is more honesty there. They can allow themselves to be honest, because if the lover cannot accept them for what they are, they can always return to the marriage partner.

It is also the reason why prostitution will never be stamped out by legislation. Certain men need the services of a call girl in order to release their pent-up tension by indulging in the sexual games they dare not play at home. And this is why I am amused when I hear or read the well-intentioned, self-elected guardians of public morality saying the police should prosecute the men who use prostitutes, instead of the girls. Apparently they are unaware that the prostitute prevents many a marriage from finishing up in the divorce courts.

In a curious way the disciples of permissiveness also fail to see the implications behind it. They claim it is a healthy manifestation and do not realize its existence springs from our sexual repression, and is therefore not a sign of tolerant maturity, but a barometer showing the growing number of people who are sexually crippled.

The illustrated, do-it-yourself sex manuals which tell the readers fifty different positions are offering them hope that if they try them all, one of them will give them the sexual pleasure they have been missing.

Hard-core pornography permits the reader to release his or her own phantasies as they read or see others doing all the things they feel would give them satisfaction.

Wife-swapping and group-sex parties allow some couples to escape from the trap they are enmeshed in, and the availability of sexual aids such as vibrators, dildoes and male prosthetic devices which let the impotent man satisfy his wife with an artificial, erect penis, has restored part sexual functioning to untold thousands.

From a psychological viewpoint this aspect of the permissive society is therapeutic, but the fact that its existence is necessary is the real tragedy.

Chapter 7
The breakdown of marriage

In spite of the continued upward spiralling of the divorce rate figures young people are still rushing into the bonds of wedlock like demented lemmings bent upon their own destruction, as they try to rejoin an emotional umbilical cord which has been severed prematurely.

They see the human contact provided by love and marriage as giving them a sense of security, and a completeness that can only be obtained when they know they are totally loved and belong to another person.

Young lovers of any age seek the safety of physical contact whenever they can. They hold hands, sit side by side in close physical communion, play 'footsie' under the table when they are sitting next to or opposite each other, and if they cannot establish contact in these ways their fingers will lingeringly touch as a drink is passed or a cigarette is lit.

They are able to communicate non-verbally with their eyes and it is their physical and mental *togetherness* which gives them the courage to let down some of their defences.

Their ability to communicate surrounds them with an aura of invulnerability, and it is the latter which gave rise to the saying that 'love is blind'. But if it is then 'marriage is the therapy which restores sight'. This may sound to be cynical, although it is not meant to be. It is a statement that is at present unfortunately all too true for most.

The parents of the young men and women contemplating marriage have already learned that love, as the youngsters experience it, will not last, and they attempt to talk them out of it by saying, 'You are much too young. Why not enjoy being single for a time? There is plenty of time for you to settle down in a few years from now. So why waste your youth?'

Lovers ignore the advice and counselling. They prefer to ignore the statistics which show that a large percentage of young marriages end up in the divorce court. They are sure their love will last, unlike that of their parents which has faded away into a meaningless relationship comprising two people living together, but sharing little.

A well known psychologist wrote to me, 'By its very nature, marriage is deceitful. This deceit – lying if we are going to give it its proper name – is inherent in the marriage contract. It is destructive. All lying eventually destroys the soul, and to stay married it is necessary to lie. For this reason, the purchase of the marriage licence – the first step in the marriage contract – is a licence to destroy.' And the man who wrote those words is not an embittered misogynist, he is a married man!

The immediate reaction to this doctor's assessment of marriage is to dismiss it as preposterous, and the response is understandable because the majority of married couples equate dishonesty with sexual infidelity. They assume that when a husband or wife finds and takes a lover, it is the third person which breaks up a hitherto happy marriage. This is incorrect. The lover is not the cause of any breakdown, he or she is a product of marital deceit and is an attempt to escape from dishonesty.

Let me make it clear, neither the psychologist nor I are implying that people enter the matrimonial state with the deliberate intention of basing their relationship upon dishonesty, but a careful and prolonged study has shown that most marriages do disintegrate into a state of uneasy neutrality, with mutual deception as a basic component.

But why does marriage contain within itself the seeds of its own destruction? Why has the American witticism appeared, 'The reason why people marry is so that they will have someone to divorce'? And what happens to the young lovers with their honest communication to turn them into deceitful, married people?

To arrive at any concrete answers each question has to be dealt with in turn. 'You never know anyone until you have lived with them', provides an initial clue.

Due to the fear of committing any act, or saying anything,

which would result in our rejection, all of us have developed what Professor Freud called the 'ego' which protects the secret part of ourselves which we, again through fear of non-acceptance, have learned to rarely share with anyone else, and if we do honour them with such a confidence we never completely reveal everything.

The late movie maker Walt Disney brought to the screen the story of *Ferdinand, the bull with the delicate ego*, who would rather spend his time appreciating the beauty of nature and the perfumes of the flowers, than going into the bullring to gore a matador to death.

Audiences everywhere hailed it as an amusing film, but all who saw it, and those who did not, have a large part of Ferdinand in their personality make-up. Deep inside ourselves we have a self-concept of what we are really like if only we had the opportunity to be ourselves.

While sitting in the office from nine to five o'clock each day we know that our real self is identical to James Bond, and we only await the opportunity to rescue a series of beautiful girls from indescribable perils, seduce them with masculine abandon, and then board a jet-plane bound for new adventures on a different continent.

If we are not James Bond, we are a famous research chemist who has discovered a cure for a previously incurable illness, and are internationally fêted for our services to mankind; an engineer building a bridge over a deep and dangerous gorge in the heart of Africa, or an explorer finding the Lost City in the Amazonian jungle.

As the dishes are being washed or the house is being vacuumed, we are really an attractive air hostess without any ties, who flies from country to country, meeting people and enjoying seeing the world; a modern Mata Hari who uses her feminine charms to obtain the enemy's secrets, thereby saving our country, but due to the secrecy implicit in our profession, never receiving public recognition for our services; or a Brigitte Bardot sought after and fought for by millions of men.

It does not matter what our daydreams are, we have them. They are part of our ego, and are vital to us. For once we lose our dreams of what we will do one day in the future, the years ahead become barren and meaningless, and death alone awaits our arrival.

Once the importance of daydreaming is recognized, the men and women in their forties who have an extra-marital relationship with a younger person can be understood. They are not going through a phase and indulging themselves in a last sexual fling to recapture their lost youth, after which they will return to the marriage bed having got it out of their system. They have reached a point where they realize their dreams for the future will never be attained unless they escape from the thwarting bonds of wedlock, and as most of them cannot make personal decisions, and implement them, they elect to remain married and forget about their daydreams, with the resulting psychological and psychosomatic illnesses.

A more striking example of the importance of having daydreams for the future is seen in the aged, senior citizen's apparent loss of memory.

Towards the end of her life my mother could not recall what had been said to her after a short period and this was attributed to a natural decline of her mental faculties. With old age she and others like her are supposed to suffer the destruction of the memory cells in the brain. Yet this explanation is not wholly correct. When I asked my mother what had happened to her some twenty-five years earlier, for instance on Armistice Day 1918, when she was a serving member of the WAACs in France, she showed me that her memory was as good as ever by describing the most minute details of the celebration.

As my mother's memory was not an isolated case I was forced into accepting that the inability of the aged to recall the minor events of the present is because they know their lives are coming to an end, and the future is not for them. Everything of importance which is going to happen has already happened, hence their living in the past awaiting death.

However the ego's need to protect our real and secret self cannot be held entirely responsible for the lying and deceit which leads to the destruction of love and its replacement by tolerated frustration. The sense of ownership conferred upon each partner by the marriage ceremony has to be considered.

In the beginning the lovers have the desire to belong one to another and to recreate the attachment of infancy. But once the legally binding formalities are completed their attitudes can undergo a change. For one thing there is not the same necessity to act as much as before, and some aspects of the personality which were repressed to prevent the courtship from floundering are permitted to surface and the partner finds a partial stranger in the house.

Another is the erroneous idea that getting married will, by a miraculous process, change the personality of the partner for the better. 'Don't worry, dear. He will change once you are married and have a home of your own', is the advice given to girls by their mothers. Whether this is actually said is unimportant, because both newly-weds are apt to try and make the other into what they consider as their ideal man or woman. Consideration for one another is replaced by a subtle power struggle to decide who is going to rule the roost and the manoeuvring blocks the free-flow of conversation.

To preserve some individuality the lying begins. At first these are about unimportant things, but as the psychologist said earlier, 'All lying destroys the soul.'

'What are you thinking about?' the man asks his wife as she sits deeply engrossed in thought. This is an invasion of the wife's inner, private world, and she protects it by lying. 'Nothing, dear', she answers.

Her husband knows she is lying, and he resents being excluded from her thoughts. 'You must have been thinking about something. Come on, tell me what it was.'

He wants to share everything with her. He does not want a repetition of his exclusion from his mother.

The thought pattern may have been quite trivial, but could cause a minor scene, so she compounds the lie, 'I was just thinking about what housework I had to do tomorrow.'

Again the husband knows she is lying, and it is not long before he stops asking.

Nor is it a one-sided exclusion. His wife asks when he gets home, 'And what did you do today?' as she is interested in what her husband does, and wants to share things with him.

'Nothing much', is the stock answer presented in various ways, because nothing unusual has happened. But the wife still wants to know and presses further.

'I told you. It was just another day, and not worth talking about,' he snaps back, and picks up the newspaper and buries his head in it, or switches on the television.

The wife has bought a new dress for a party they are going to, and she puts it on and asks, 'Do you like it? Do you think it will be all right for tonight?'

He thinks it does not suit her, but he prefers not to hurt her or start an argument so he lies. 'Yes, it is very nice.'

Aware of the insincerity in his voice she tries to get his real opinion. 'Do you really like it? Tell me the truth.'

Forced into compounding the earlier untruth he becomes a little annoyed. 'I have just told you it is very nice. So shut up and get dressed, otherwise we will be late.'

At the party they both meet a person of the opposite sex they find attractive, and as they drive home the wife, having noticed how her husband, John, was enjoying the other woman's company, puts out a verbal feeler. 'What did you think of Sandra?' she enquires casually.

'Which one was Sandra?' he counters.

His wife recognizes the lie-game they are playing, but is not deterred and describes Sandra.

'Oh her,' John says, putting a touch of surprise into his voice, implying she was not important enough to remember. 'All right I suppose, but not my type.'

They both know John is lying, and being embarrassed at the invasion of his privacy he retaliates with, 'And what did you think of Richard?'

She interprets the question correctly, as a way of telling her to mind her own business, and she quickly formulates a non-reply, 'He was all right, but typical. He has been successful in everything he has done, including with women, and he spent all the time talking about himself. Gosh! I'm tired. Are you ready for bed?'

Her answer conveys an unspoken apology, and after being equally untruthful she turns the conversation into an acceptable area of discussion.

Neither can admit that as normal human beings they will be constantly finding themselves attracted to people of the opposite sex, but the fact that they are attracted does not mean they are going to jump into bed with them at the earliest opportunity. Should one of them admit he or she finds someone else attractive it can lead to an accusation of disloyalty, and so married couples are secretly disloyal and imagine, as they are having sexual intercourse that night, they are making love to the person they had met earlier.

And the reason why men stop talking about their daydreams for the future is because wives fail to appreciate that they are only wishes; that it is unimportant whether they materialize and to seal the silence, in moments of anger, wives say, 'Well, why don't you do something about it. You are always talking about what you are going to do, but you never do anything, and that is typical of you.'

It is due to the initial small white lies, plus each partner trying to protect the other, and their establishment of neutral areas for discussion, that they lose the art of real communication and build up a barrier between themselves.

These imaginary conversations and situations show why and how the lying commences, but have done little more than scratch the surface. The reasons why people marry when they are young are just as important.

To some young men and women marriage is a means of establishing their adulthood, and escaping from parental control. If this is the underlying motive it is hardly surprising that the new adult who emerges after marriage has the desire to do things which are incompatible with the marital state.

If either lacks sexual experience, and has not experimented in the Don Juan phase of their emotional development, marriage can well be the magic wand that awakens them from adolescent slumber and make them inquisitive about making love to someone else. It may also give them the adult confidence to explore that avenue of experimental wonderment, hence the large number of comparatively newly-married people who have an extramarital relationship. The affair has nothing to do with the love they have for each other, because it is their love which provides them with the confidence and security to enter into it, but this can lead them into the divorce court.

Should the couple be emotionally immature the marriage provides the atmosphere for them to grow up, and when that occurs the partner who matures will alter. His or her attitudes will change and with newly acquired confidence he or she will embark upon an entirely different and successful career where the spouse will be unnecessary.

A sign of male and female immaturity becomes noticeable during the nine months of pregnancy and immediately after the baby is born. The man who has been starved of parental contact and affection finds it difficult to accept the fact that his wife is pregnant, and that in a few months there will be a baby in the home making demands upon her. Unconsciously he resents the unborn child because its demands for attention and affection are the things he still needs, for he is an emotional baby trying to recapture the lost past. Quite unconsciously he feels his wife has betrayed him and is nurturing a usurper in her womb. He then has to prove to himself that he is wanted, and as his wife does not give him that proof he looks for another woman who will. If his wife does not recognize the symptoms and makes too much fuss over their child when it is born, or they have two or three children quickly and they are all demanding attention, then he sees the only course of action open to him is to leave her for the other woman.

The woman who unconsciously equates her husband with an all-loving, pandering father begins reacting towards the end of pregnancy and after the baby is born. She turns against her husband for making her pregnant, for making her into a mother, because she still wants to be treated as the only child. Then with the birth of the baby her animosity is expressed against the infant by treating it as a nuisance. She starts going out with her single women friends in search of a man who will treat her as a child rather than a mother.

Should the husband challenge her about her behaviour, and suggest she spends more time at home with him and the baby the animosity is verbalized: 'It is all right for you. You are out at work all day, mixing with other people, but I am cooped up in the house with the baby all day long. I have to get out for a while otherwise I would go mad. And there is no reason why I should stay at home all the time. I'm still young. Having a baby doesn't make me into an old woman. And it is not as if I were abandoning the child leaving no one to look after it. You are here, and you are just as responsible for it as I am. . . .'

An entire volume could be written about the effects of primal deprivation upon married couples, but as far as I am concerned in this book the object is to show how marriage can create the stress it should relieve.

But before coming to the end of the chapter, there is another important reason why young people have a compulsion to marry, and that is their need to own and control the object of their love.

Through adolescence they have searched for love like a frenzied alcoholic searching for the last bottle he has hidden too well. At times they think they have found it, but as they bask in the security the love gives them there is a thought constantly nagging away at the back of their mind, 'It is too good to last. Something is bound to happen to take my happiness away.'

Their fear is a direct throw-back to their infancy when they were given limited mother-child contact, and once they feel that something is going to happen, they cannot tolerate the uncertainty, and deliberately destroy the thing, the love they want.

Of course the chances are that they would lose their lover anyway because they are more in love with love than a living person. When the living man or woman does anything the romanticized ideal would never do, their fears become justified and the sword of Damocles does fall to sever the relationship.

In either case they are sure they will never love again. They are heart-broken. And it is true they never will love in the same way again, because each love is unique. But at the time they do not appreciate that their need to love will drive them to find a new lover. All they are really aware of is, 'If I ever fall in love again I am going to make certain that it lasts', and the legal marriage ceremony is seized upon as the answer.

This may sound old-fashioned and inapplicable to our liberated youth, but it is not. An eighteen-year-old student in her first year of training to be a teacher announced to her father that she wanted to get married, and as the legal age of consent was then twenty-one she needed his written consent.

Her father tried to be practical about his daughter's future and he expressed his doubts about the wisdom of her getting married during her first year at college. 'As a wife you will have to consider your husband's future as well as your own, and as he is planning to go to university shortly I feel there is a good chance you will leave college, if you marry, before the end of your course. I would prefer you to finish the three years, get your teacher's certificate, and then if anything happens in the future you can always support yourself.'

As he considered he had a modern outlook on sex, and because he was talking to a modern-thinking girl with a modern-thinking boyfriend, the father proposed that his daughter get an apartment in the town where the college was located and live together.

'During your vacations you can both come and live at home if you want to. Then at the end of your three years at college you will be twenty-one years old, and can make up your own mind about legalizing your relationship.'

His daughter thought it was a good idea and promised to talk it over with her boyfriend. But his reaction to the proposal was something the father did not expect. According to the daughter in a later conversation his reply was, 'The dirty old bastard. I want you to be mine.'

In those few words can be seen the young man's need to establish 'ownership' over the love-object.

For the record, the outcome of this quoted episode was that the father agreed to the marriage and it took place shortly after his daughter left college. Happily the marriage has been a success as the husband has since found he does not have to own and control his wife to ensure her continued love.

After examining people's attempts to cope with the marital situation there cannot be any doubt that due to anxiety the institution of marriage is breaking down. But the pessimistic view of the psychologist that, 'by its very nature, marriage is deceitful...' is a fallacy.

People everywhere want to be loved and to love within a permanent relationship. Every week millions of men and women read romantic stories and watch romantic plays and films on television, and are upset if they do not have a happy ending. They want to be happily married, but they cannot see how to jump over the hurdles they have unconsciously created and attain the true union of a man and a woman they know can and must exist.

Chapter 8
Ways to surmount the marital hurdles

To avoid any confusion in the mind of the reader it is necessary to define the difference I make between *phantasies* and *daydreams*.

Daydreams are the plans for the future which we hope to achieve one day, and they are essential to human well-being. They are the food of personal and social development, without which there would be no progress.

Phantasies, on the other hand, are the things we would like to happen now to make our present existence more enjoyable. They are restrictive and poison our systems, because they prevent us from living our lives fully in the here and now.

A married couple in their twenties went to see a psychotherapist as they both recognized their marriage was becoming stale and failing.

Initially they were seen together by the therapist, then separately, and when they were alone each one said virtually the same thing. 'We seem to have lost our ability to communicate effectively, and this means there isn't any proper verbal communication and our sexual communication is nil. We are simply drifting apart.'

There was nothing unusual about them. On the contrary, most married couples go through the same phase. But the majority accept it as something which is bound to happen once the first flush of love has faded.

The therapist agreed to continue seeing them individually each week to assist them in obtaining insight into their personal hang-ups, but asked them to apply while they were at home a modified form of 'co-counselling' on every alternate day.

This meant, for half-an-hour every other day they were to sit down facing each other, preferably on the floor and not too far apart, and decide who was going to speak first.

Having made the decision the 'talker' was to use fifteen minutes to talk about anything he or she felt to be important. How their partner was affecting them, what was upsetting them, etc., and if nothing came to mind the time should be spent relating what had happened during the day and how they felt about those events.

The 'listener' was to really listen for the quarter of an hour without assessing what the talker was referring to, and had to stop themselves from formulating mental questions and answers about what was being said. The listener was to give undivided attention. At the end of fifteen minutes the roles were to be reversed, and the listener to become the talker.

Any topic could be explored, the only provisos being that it must not be an answer to, or a defence against what had been said before, and there were to be no verbal postmortems afterwards.

What happened to the couple as they instigated the programme, and how it progressed, will inform others of what they can expect if they too decide to surmount their hurdles of non-communication.

A little embarrassed they both sat on the floor about three feet apart.

'Which one of us is going to start? Would you like to?' Julie asked.

The husband was non-commital. 'Not really. Why don't you.'

Faced with no other alternative the woman agreed. She started to talk about neutral topics, then began to dry up, and it was on the point of fizzling out into a lesson on how not to communicate when the doorbell rang to announce the unexpected arrival of some friends for a visit.

Julie told her therapist the next time they met, 'I didn't know what to talk about. There was a lot I wanted to say, and there still is, but I couldn't get it out in case what I said hurt him.'

After their friends had left and they were in bed, they agreed to have another attempt the next day, but the next day neither of them mentioned it. Julie described her attitude as, 'George had agreed to try it again, so I wasn't going to push it. I felt the onus was on him to make the first move.'

George did not refer to it and he made a point, when he got home in the evening of settling down in front of the television set and watching it until it was time to go to bed. These tactics annoyed his wife, and a few days later she suggested they try again. Her husband readily agreed to try the following night, and when Julie challenged him about his silence his reply was, 'I thought it better if you decided whether you wanted to go ahead and do it. I didn't want to force you into anything.'

That was George's turn to try and remain upon neutral ground to protect his wife's feelings, and most probably his own as well. But the following night they adhered to the suggested routine, and began to see results.

Julie summed up her reactions, 'I started off by talking about nothing in particular, trivia, but after a couple of minutes I couldn't keep that up. I told him how I felt about all sorts of things. I would start telling him about one thing, and that reminded me of something else. In the beginning I was worried about how George would take what I was saying, so I watched his face closely, and do you know, he was listening to me. He was trying to understand how I felt and wasn't on the defensive at all. Yes, he was really listening. Gosh, it was good to be able to talk like that.'

George gave his assessment of the same session the next time he visited the therapist. 'I didn't feel like talking much, so I told Julie what I had done throughout the day and how I had felt about the things which had happened.

'I know there were a lot of things I could have talked about, but when my fifteen minutes were over Julie said to me, "That is the first time you have ever told me what has happened to you during the day, and it was great. I felt you were at last sharing your life with me." I did not realize,' George said, 'that that sort of thing would interest her.'

With the progression of weeks the frequency of the co-counselling sessions was reduced to one a week of an hour's duration, and the couple discovered there were at least three tangible benefits. They found the confidence to use their counselling time to talk about the many things which had remained repressed over the years.

They began talking to each other about meaningful subjects during the remainder of the week, and the television set was not used as often as an escape from verbal contact. Their sexual activity became more prolific, and recovered some of its lost spontaneity.

The original idea of co-counselling was conceived in the United States by Harvey Jackins of Seattle, Washington, and now there are thousands of groups meeting regularly throughout America and in Britain to practise 're-evaluation counselling'.[1]

Jackins recognized the lack of communication as a problem besetting our technological age and advocated that people should meet in groups each week, choose a partner, decide who was going to be the talker and the listener, and for an hour each talk about the things they had experienced in the past which had left a definite impression on them.

The theory of re-evaluation counselling is based upon the hypothesis that past experiences affect the present mode of life if the emotions they produced were not fully released at the time or released later. The emotions evoked do not fade away with the passing of time, they remain locked within the body-structure and colour the way a person currently feels, acts and thinks. When a situation which is similar to the one in the past is met with, the repressed emotions are activated, preventing the event from being dealt with in a rational manner.

On this side of the Atlantic, entirely independent from Harvey Jackins, Dr Rachel Pinney arrived at the conclusion that there is a crying need for 'creative listening', and in a paper published under that name she outlines why the need exists:

In political and other controversies both sides think they are right and attempt to convince their opponents. The results of this are well known. Far from being converted or modified in their views, both sides become hardened in their own faith/prejudice, and the rift is increased, not decreased. View modification rarely takes place.

Conferences, committees and breakfast tables, especially if including children, foreign language speakers or the deaf, are full of not-heard communications, interruptions and frustrated would-be communicators.

[1] See *The Human Side of Human Beings: The Theory of Re-Evaluation Counselling*, Rational Island Publishers, Seattle, USA.

An eager *why*-asking two-year-old turns into a homework-reluctant teenager. Young children are constantly clamouring for attention, and when they receive it, it is more often than not part attention which does not satisfy, but increases the need for full attention. . . .[2]

During a recent conversation Dr Pinney told me an anecdote which illustrates how a man and wife at the breakfast table can, unwittingly, reinforce non-communication and rejection. She asked me to imagine that we were married, and one morning after I had taken the last piece of toast she became very upset, which led to my storming out of the house.

That evening she asked if I would listen to how she felt about my taking the piece of toast. I agreed, lit my pipe, and settled down in an armchair.

'When you took that piece of toast,' she explained, 'I felt like a little girl again, and you were my father. Yes, I was back to being a little girl, and I remembered vividly all the anger and frustration I felt as he took the last piece of toast, and I allowed how I felt then to be expressed this morning.'

With a loud sucking noise, meant to convey understanding and sympathy, I replied, 'I know exactly how you felt. It was the same for me last week when there wasn't a cup of coffee left for me.'

Dr Pinney explained how I, the imaginary husband, had not conveyed understanding and sympathy. By taking her experience and relating it to myself and the cup of coffee, I had stopped her from a continuing communication, and subtly rejected her. For if I had been a 'creative listener' who wanted to communicate with my wife, I would have seen the significance of what she was saying and encouraged her to go back to the breakfast incident with her father to find out why she was angry with him, thereby releasing the pent-up tension.

As the frustration through non-communication starts in childhood, Dr Pinney recommends that all children be given a regular 'watch me' hour, when the child can do and talk about whatever he likes, and the adult does not attempt to join in, unless invited to, but agrees to listen carefully to what he is saying or doing.

[2] *Creative Listening*, Creative Listening Ltd., Springlong, Loddington, Kettering, Northants., June 1970.

The 'watch me' period is open to free movement and expression, and the adult encourages this by saying in appropriate words, 'You can do anything you like, and I'll see you don't burn the house down, throw me out of the window, or annoy the neighbours too much.'

Over the last twelve years Rachel Pinney has been applying this to children. She comments, 'It is interesting to note that there is not a word in the English language to describe the listening taking place. It is more than observing, it is more than listening. Every child recognizes it at once as something he has a need for....' and '*A child receiving such an hour changes. A growth releasing process has taken place.*'[3]

An American trained psychiatrist now practising in London, Dr Jerome Liss, MD, believes in the natural healing capacity of the individual once they have discharged all the frustrated emotions through various 'growth techniques', but primarily through 'co-operative help'.

In his manual *Co-Operative Help: The Art of Helpful Listening*,[4] he explains how his adaptation of Harvey Jackins's method can be used by man-to-wife, parent-to-child, and all the other combinations of a one-to-one relationship, and gives his explanation as to the therapeutic value.

For instance, people are always interrupting a conversation before it reaches its logical conclusion, and:

This inhibits or fragments thoughts and stops up feelings which remain as undischarged tensions. . . . There is a special and delightful growth process when one is patiently attended to by a receptive listener, when one can think out or feel in silence the fragments of disconnected experience, and know that whatever one says from this silence will be gladly received.[5]

Dr Liss admits that co-operative help resembles Freudian catharsis – permitting a patient to verbally purge himself in the sanctuary of the psychoanalyst's office. But instead of the analyst playing the part of a psychological superman and giving his, the analyst's, interpretations of what the patient really means, the

[3] *Creative Listening*, page 8. Emphasis added by the author.
[4] Published by Jerome Liss, MD, London.
[5] Ibid., page 8.

talker does it all for himself, and the 'emotional discharge means emotional learning and this means emotional change'.[6]

He summed up the process concisely when he wrote, 'Carl Jung has said we become sick because we keep secrets. Co-operative help aims at reaching and disclosing one's private thoughts. Once revealed the steam is taken out, further considerations soothe them and the pressure is off.'[7]

Couples finding they can talk through co-counselling can re-establish meaningful sexuality, like Julie and George, but it must remain non-orgasmic as long as either of them have unexpressed phantasies festering inside their minds. As long as one or the other sexual partner is phantasizing during coitus there cannot be the free expression indispensable for the complete orgasm. The man cannot cry out the name of the phantasized lover because that would insult his wife. The woman who is pretending her phantasy consort is doing to her all the physical things which she feels would make intercourse more pleasurable, can obtain no sense of gratification, because the reality person is performing the act in his usual way.

It does not matter what the phantasy is, rape, troilism, wife-swapping, masochism, etc., the mental energy it produces remains undischarged as long as it is a secret, and its potency continues building up until it reaches a near flash-point where the phantasy has to be consummated with another partner, or the victim of the phantasy is forced into becoming asexual, as he or she fears they will not be able to control it if sexual intercourse takes place with their marriage partner.

Both eventualities produce further tensions. The husband who finds a woman prepared to accept and respond to his sexual extravaganza may feel such a tremendous relief that, what started off as a casual affair becomes a permanent dependency, and he is forced into living a double life. The woman who becomes asexual has to reject the advances of her husband in self-protection, thus creating a deeper breach between them.

A woman I saw with symptoms of apparent frigidity had been forced into becoming asexual through her wish to be physically

6 Ibid., page 7.
7 Ibid., page 15.

hurt during intercourse. She felt she could not tell her husband about her desires as she knew it would inform him she had masochistic tendencies. It was a long time before she could tell me what the trouble was, but after talking about it and exploring what it meant as far as she was concerned, plus its origins – how as a child she had been taught to regard sex as dirty and as an adult made it acceptable by being punished during her indulgence – the phantasy was dissipated and ceased to threaten her. Had this client been able to talk to her husband there would have been no need for her to see a therapist.

In writing the last paragraph, however, I have been guilty of over simplifying the issues involved. Sexual problems have correctly been called the silent plague of the twentieth century, and whereas there is a lot of superficial talk about it, supplemented by books galore, it is difficult to discuss the matter openly with the only person who is important, the sexual partner. That is why I have found co-counselling to be a pre-requisite. It enables other subjects to be ventilated and shows the man and wife that their difficulties are those of the individual, and not a reflection upon their spouse. Only when meaningful conversation has been established should the couple start approaching sexual communication in 'This is what I would like' sessions.

These require both of them to sit naked on the floor, about three feet apart, and make the first decision, 'Who is going to start talking about what they would like to happen?' But having made the decision it does not imply that sexual intercourse has to take place. It can, and frequently does, but it must always be spontaneous rather than planned.

For that reason whoever commences prefaces what they are going to say by, 'When we next make love I would like . . .', and then they can talk about the things which are uppermost in their mind at the moment. At the end they ask, 'Now what would you like to do?' Until that moment the companion remains silent and unmoving. Then it is their turn to talk.

Often the wishes are quite different, but somehow because of the frankness of the disclosures they match up without any conscious planning, giving both satisfaction. Should the occasion arise when the suggestions are unacceptable, the partner should refrain from saying 'I don't like the idea of doing that' when it is their turn to talk, as the words amount to a rejection, preventing further personal growth. Mirror it back as Dr Cohen does. Get the talker to explore it further by asking, 'You said you would like to . . ., and before I tell you what I would like to happen, could you tell me why it appeals to you?'

The answer can do two things. As the motive underlying it is thought over and put into words the desire can diminish. Alternatively it can make the wish more agreeable, and even if neither happens it does not matter, for the rule of these sessions is that they are aimed at what people would like to happen, instead of a demand.

If the sexual honesty involved does not culminate in intercourse, and as I have written it is not vital to the marital therapy, it can leave one or other aroused, without an opportunity for release. A woman found that she was in such a position, and as she had no intention of permitting herself to be frustrated as she had done previously, she said to her husband, 'Darling, I feel you don't want to make love, and I don't want you to feel you have to just to please me, but I am feeling sexy, and am going to masturbate!'

When she discussed it later with her therapist she told him that her husband's response had made her feel marvellous. He did not interpret it as rejection as he formerly did when she failed to achieve an orgasm. Instead he put his arms around her, and showed her, by the warmth of his embrace, that he understood.

'That was a breakthrough for us both,' she said to her therapist. 'When I wanted sex in the past and he didn't, he used to force himself to satisfy me, but I felt guilty because he was only doing what he thought was his duty. I used to ask myself if I were too over-sexed for him, but since that day there have been times when one of us wanted to make love and the other didn't, and neither of us pretend any more. We masturbate.'

At various seminars and lectures I have given I have been frequently faced with questions about masturbation. Is it safe to indulge in it? Don't people become addicted to it? Can anyone masturbate to excess? And a host of other queries. These used to surprise me as I thought we had outgrown the myth that it caused everything from spots to blindness, insanity, baldness, and hairs in the palm of a man's hand, and my answers were flippant. But the questioners were serious and now I treat the questions seriously.

The American sex researcher, the late Dr Alfred C. Kinsey, and his colleagues at Indiana University, gathered data which proved that nearly all men had masturbated, and over 60 per cent of women had as well, and there was a rise in the frequency curve as men and women reached their middle forties. They also confirmed that, despite popular notions, it is not detrimental to health.[8]

Nor can it be practised to excess, because the body protects itself. Men find they do not obtain an erection, and women find there are no pleasurable sensations left in the genital area. And no well-adjusted person can become addicted to it, to the exclusion of hetero-sexual activity, unless the relationship has deteriorated so badly that phantasies alone dominate their sexual interests.

But to return to co-counselling. Those couples who have used it until communication was re-established, and then extended it into 'This is what I would like' sessions, have automatically begun talking about their phantasies, permitting the release of energy formerly bound up in them and an expansion of their previously restricted personalities.

[8] Alfred C. Kinsey, and others, *Sexual Behaviour in the Human Male* and *Sexual Behaviour in the Human Female*, W. B. Saunders Co. Ltd., London, 1948 and 1953.

Chapter 9
The under-developed personality

The story of Peter Pan, the little boy who never grew up, has had popular appeal since J. M. Barrie created him seventy-odd years ago, and for good reason. All of us recognize a part of ourselves in Peter.

What has not been appreciated is that the element of childishness is often a sign of arrested development, and is not confined to the personality, but is reflected in the body structure and the way the body functions.

I began to come to this conclusion back in the early 1960s when I was working on my thesis 'Three Phases of the Mind-Body Relationship'. This entailed a study of women who were unable to conceive, adopted a child, and shortly afterwards became pregnant, and observing the women who had repeated, spontaneous terminations of pregnancy.

What I wanted to discover was, what were the personality factors which prevented conception and motherhood? Once they were pin-pointed, could the same mechanics be duplicated, by hypnotic suggestion, to prevent unwanted pregnancies, and to be a more effective method of natural birth control?

The sample I used to test out my hypothesis of hypnotic birth control was too small to provide anything but tentative conclusions. It comprised six married, Roman Catholic couples whose religious beliefs made artificial contraception unacceptable. They had already tried using the rhythm method of birth control without success, and had two or more children.

The women underwent a series of sessions where, in the hypnotic state, their menstrual periods were first regularized into a regular monthly cycle. While still in hypnosis they were then given the appropriate suggestions to the effect that as they already had children and did not want any more at the moment, their bodies would respect their wishes; they would be able to enjoy sexual intercourse with the full knowledge that they had no need, reason or desire to conceive, and their periods would continue to start at a regular time of the month. None of the women in the small group became pregnant during the year I followed up their progress.[1]

As there was no control group – six other couples who simply went ahead having normal sexual intercourse without any contraceptive aids, including hypnotic suggestion – there was no way I could ascertain with any degree of accuracy how many of the women in my sample might have conceived in the same twelve months, thereby allowing me to be more positive about the outcome.

However, a number of interesting things did emerge from the research. The women I worked with who were unable to conceive were all suffering from arrested emotional development, a condition I later referred to as 'the little girl syndrome'. In hypnoanalysis all of them revealed episodes in their childhood which unconsciously prevented them from being mature women and mothers. Consciously, and in some cases physically, they were poised ready to assume a fully adult, feminine role as a mother, but they needed an extra undefinable 'something' to free them from their childhood personality impediment.

The releasing agency did not have to be psychotherapy for all women. Motherhood by adoption could be sufficient for the woman to throw off her fears and subsequently conceive, and a recent newspaper report showed that a symbol can be equally effective.

The *Sunday Express*[2] reported how a lady who had been childless for six years bought a gold fertility doll for £5 when she was out in West Africa. Within a month of wearing the doll on a bracelet she became pregnant, and six other women who borrowed the doll from her also became mothers.

The owner of the doll told a *Sunday Express* reporter, 'There are people who will laugh and say it is rubbish. But can they be

[1] A summary of the thesis was circulated under the title *Hyp-No-Birth*, meant to stimulate interest among the general public, in 1964.
[2] Issue dated 14 November 1971.

sure? A doctor told me that wearing it might help childless women by relieving their tension. It certainly worked with me, and it worked with six others.'[3]

And having written earlier that only some of the barren women I worked with were ready, physically, to assume adult motherhood, I have to add that the majority retained a 'little girl' figure, with the under-developed bust of the post-pubescent child.

Recognizing the significance of the small bust, and how many women want to increase their chest measurements, I asked myself the question, 'Could the size of the bust be increased by locating and removing the remnants of childhood, existing in the unconscious mind and preventing physical maturity?'

Before I had time to delve into the answer the long arm of coincidence stretched out and touched me on the shoulders in the shape of Mr Mohammed Ali Mirza, a hypnotherapist of forty years' experience, practising in Blackpool, Lancashire. I mentioned to him the line of inquiry I intended to follow and he most generously told me what he had done in the same area. A thirty-year-old woman had gone to see him after reading an advertisement he had placed in a local paper stating that he could help people to slim by taking away excess weight, or help them to gain weight. She asked Mr Mirza if he could increase the size of her bust which, to use her own words 'was quite flat'. The hypnotist agreed to try it as an experiment. 'In about three months I put on two-and-a-half inches,' she delightedly told a newspaper reporter.

Another lady aged thirty-three years heard about the results while she was sitting in Mr Mirza's waiting room, and she gained two inches within two months.

Again by word of mouth, a twenty-five-year-old mother of a baby girl learned what was happening and, 'after four sessions of hypnosis I gained two inches and I'm keeping the treatment up.'

A national newspaper provided details of the method Mr Mirza used. He saw each woman once a fortnight. 'I put her in a deep

[3] By quoting this case from the *Sunday Express* I am not suggesting, because I have no way of knowing, that this particular lady was suffering from the 'little girl syndrome'.

trance', he explained. 'All I did was to tell her that her bust would get bigger. And it did.' When asked to give an explanation for the phenomena, Mr Mirza told a reporter that he personally believed the mind can do anything, even control the glands.[4]

In that statement I think Mirza over-simplified the issues involved. My subsequent findings show that hypnosis does not necessarily control the glands in this particular instance; rather suggestions given in the hypnotic state permit the glands to throw off unconscious restraints, and function properly, possibly for the first time as an adult.

Since the day Mr Mirza and I met I have worked with a large number of flat-chested women, and it has become a regular part of my practice. Some of the women have been single girls in their early twenties, and others have been married women with ages ranging up to forty-six years.

Their case-histories are as individual as the people themselves. A percentage had always had a small bust, and having children had not affected the size of the bust one way or another. Others found that their busts became fuller after the birth of their first child, but after the second or third they became small again. A number of them had had well formed breasts before they had any children, only to find that after their first child was born the bust shrank and never regained its former fullness.

While these women were in analysis I came up with some interesting reasons why it had happened to them, but as the space available to me in this book is limited, I will put down certain generalizations.

The women whose breasts had always been small in comparison to their overall measurements had, for the most part, unresolved 'little girl' unconscious conflicts, and the smallness of their busts expressed their need to remain and be treated with the love and consideration they wanted as a child, but had not got. Helped to gain insight into these underlying problems, most of them managed to escape from the ties of wanting to still be a child and developed both a mature personality, and a mature bust.

[4] Details of Mr Mirza's work were reported in the national newspapers, *The News of the World*, 17 February 1957, the *Daily Sketch*, 18 February 1957, and others.

Those who found their breasts rounded out after the birth of their first child, only to lose their figure-form when more children arrived, found they could cope with and enjoy having a son or daughter, and it was fulfilling a need. However as the other children arrived, their earlier, unresolved childhood conflicts returned and they wanted to be treated as a child by their husbands, instead of the younger children getting all the attention and affection.

The same mental process is involved in the women who had well-formed breasts before they had children, only to find they disappeared, never to return. In their case giving birth had re-activated dormant, unfulfilled childhood needs, and this was graphically illustrated by an American lady who came to see me. She had had a baby when she was little more than a child herself; when her bust had not had the opportunity to achieve adult proportions. Since the birth of her baby the remainder of her body has continued to grow and round out, with the exception of her breasts. They were retarded at the chronological age of maturity she had reached when she became a mother.

Nor is the physical growth limited to the bust. It can and does take place long after the age when experts proclaim growth has stopped and the entire body, or parts of it, can grow.

A young woman in therapy with me for her 'little girl syndrome' found her body becoming more mature, the thighs rounding out, her hips broadening, and her bust developing without us ever specifically dealing with physical growth.

A man in his late twenties who was being treated for an anxiety state, discarded the glasses he had previously been forced to wear, put on weight, his body became manly instead of being effeminate, the hair on his head, face and body grew thicker, and all this happened once he had the confidence to face up to the fears he had been repressing.

Of course when therapists like myself make claims of this type they are considered suspect, because the reader is denied access to the case histories to protect clients' anonymity. So let us leave the realm of psychodynamics and dwell for a while in the everyday world of newspaper and magazine advertisements.

The women's journals frequently carry large advertisements

offering to increase the size of under-developed busts. How the advertisers intend to accomplish this varies: there are mechanical chest exercisers to tone up the muscles, creams and a specific massage routine, and the latest I have heard about in Britain is the 'Aqua Maid', a clear plastic shell which fits over a breast, and is attached to the water faucet. When the tap is turned on, the water is sprayed onto the breast giving it a water-massage.

While all the aids have a toning-up effect there is scant scientific evidence to prove that any of them, with the exception of surgery and hormone implants, will produce long term, positive results.

But for many of the millions of women who use them, they work, and the companies marketing them can produce thick files of genuine letters from satisfied customers, telling of increases from one-and-a-half inches upwards, or perhaps I should have written, outwards.

Men, too, are catered for in newspapers and magazines with advertisements offering special hair preparations to overcome baldness. The hair-restoring lotions sold to the hair-seekers do contain beneficial trace elements, but the inescapable fact is that science has not yet produced a cure for baldness. Be that as it may the advertisers have their filing cabinets bulging with letters and photographs of before and after from satisfied customers who are thrilled with their new shock of hair.

I talked to my father, Henry Blythe, about this as he has been a consultant hypnotist in Torquay and Gloucester for many years, and recently appeared on a nation-wide television programme devoted to hair-restoration, hypnotizing a gentleman and giving him suggestions that his hair would grow.

He told me that he had been doing this for more than twenty years, for both men and women. 'While they are in hypnosis,' he said to me, 'I place my hands upon their head, and tell them they can feel a force emanating from my hands, down to the roots of their hair. I tell them that this force is stimulating their hair to grow strongly, thickly and healthily, and I also emphasize that as they know their hair is starting to grow again they are ceasing to worry about it.'

What he said to me next was important. 'Son, if you can remove the worry about the loss of hair, there is a good chance it will begin to grow again.'

Both of these common-place examples reveal that the bust-developers and the hair-restoratives are, more or less, comparable with the gold fertility doll from West Africa.[5] If the purchaser is psychologically ready to activate, or re-activate, the growth process, and can accept the proffered aid as the key which will unlock it, they will get the required outgrowth. The difference between what I have been doing and the advertised methods is that hypno-analysis, in addition to acting as the key, allows the therapist to clean out all the accumulated rubbish from the past which could block the process up before reaching maturation.

As my own techniques were being standardized and the success rate rose I began wondering if other psychotherapists and hypnotherapists had encountered the same phenomenon. Many of them had. The late Dr Caron Kent PhD, who graduated at Königsberg in 1933, and had a distinguished career in Australia and later in Britain where he was the Director of the Highgate Clinic of Psychotherapy in London until his death in May 1971, spent most of his professional life working on unlocking the dammed-up energy, preventing full physical and psychological growth. In an article he wrote for *Character and Energy: The Journal of Bioenergetic Research*,[6] he gave a detailed case history of a hysterical twenty-three-year-old woman called Agatha. After eighteen months of therapy with him – and he did not use hypnosis – Agatha's breasts became more pronounced, her menstrual difficulties disappeared, severe personality problems were resolved, and her body took on the shape of a mature twenty-three-year-old woman.

But it was in his book *The Puzzled Body: a New Approach to the Unconscious*,[7] that Dr Kent showed how men who had broken through their childhood restrictions discovered that their penis had grown to man-size; a deformed foot and toes, the result of

[5] This statement is not meant to impugn the claims made by advertisers.
[6] Abbotsbury Publications, Abbotsbury, Dorset, Vol. 1, No. 3, September 1970.
[7] Vision Press, London, 1970.

growth being impeded by wearing too small a pair of shoes, began to grow; and many other examples of physical growth accompanied the expansion of the personality.

Out on the West Coast of America Dr Arthur Janov recorded in his book *The Primal Scream* that patients who had undergone primal therapy at his Los Angeles Institute had grown as well. A third of his flat-chested women patients wrote him about their breasts enlarging, and as this was an unexpected by-product he wrote to the patients' local doctors for verification. In all cases it was confirmed. Some of his post-primal patients grew taller, and several found their hands and feet were larger when they went to buy new gloves and shoes.

Wilhelm Reich, and Reichian therapists, had seen the same things happening thirty years ago and I discovered that an internationally known psychotherapist and author, Mr Leslie LeCron of Carmel, California, had been doing work on similar lines to my own.

Mr LeCron was asked by a young female patient if hypnosis could make her breasts grow, and he decided he would try. After three months her breasts had added two inches to their measurements. He then tried the technique on eight women. There was one complete failure due to the patient's unresolved personality problems, while the remainder had gains from one to two-and-a-half inches.

He next experimented with using women in groups, but the results were not as good as those he obtained in individual therapy, because in the group situation there was not the opportunity, or the correct therapeutic environment, to undertake hypno-analysis. His conclusions were that hypnosis could be successfully used in breast development, but the extent of breast increase could not be predetermined.[8]

How is all this possible? A few years ago, in 1968, there was a British Medical Association Clinical Meeting organized jointly with the British Paediatric Association in Cheltenham, England, and Dr Dermod MacCarthy of the Institute of Child Psychology in London told his assembled colleagues about a five-year-old boy who had not grown for a year, but grew two inches in three

[8] A published account appeared in *Forum*, Vol. 3, No. 7, 1970.

months when he was taken away from his mother and kept in hospital.

The *International Medical Tribune of Great Britain* reported Dr MacCarthy's findings:

Children rejected by their mothers may not only fail to thrive but fail to grow. . . . It was found on admission to hospital that these children had a low level of human growth hormone (HGH). But most significantly, all the symptoms, including the low levels of HGH, disappeared under hospital care. . . .[9]

Under a heading 'Unloved Children' the *Sheffield Morning Telegraph* carried a more detailed report of Dr MacCarthy's talk:

The 'unloved child syndrome' had joined the 'battered baby syndrome' to worry child-care experts, said Dr MacCarthy.

It had been known for some time that depriving a child of mother love by putting it in hospital or under impersonal institutional care for long periods cause it to fail to thrive physically as well as upset it emotionally.

But recently it has been realized that similar effects could be caused in a child living in its own home where it did not feel the warmth of love that normally flowed from mother to child. It might be that mother and child were incompatible, it might be that a new pregnancy upset the mother's relationship with her child. It could be that only one child in a family was affected. . . .[10]

Similar reports to these have been published in the United States and the literature covering this is now extensive, but recognition and acceptance of the fact that human growth hormones can be, and are, controlled by the psyche has been ignored, and people suffering from premature growth curtailment are continuing to suffer.

Now, due to the work of Reich, the neo-Reichians, Caron Kent, Arthur Janov, and others, the Peter and Petra Pans amongst us have a chance to grow up, irrespective of their age, if they wish to do so.

[9] Issue dated 7 November 1968.
[10] Issue dated 28 October 1968.

Chapter 10
Mind over matter

While I was serving ashore in the Royal Navy for a period during the Second World War there was a saying which reflected the sailors' attitude towards the meaningless discipline and the trivial tasks they were ordered to perform to keep them busy. 'If it moves, salute it, and if it doesn't move, then give it a quick coating of white paint.' Today a paraphrased version is applicable to the mechanistic approach dominating medical research, 'If it exists, then it can be measured, but if it cannot be measured, then it doesn't exist.' And this Nelsonian blind-eye outlook has been responsible for important, empirical evidence being dismissed as unworthy of investigation.

For years, if not centuries, patients and doctors alike have superficially acknowledged that the healing process, be it medical, surgical or psychological, contains within it an unknown x factor. This unquantifiable force appears so regularly that it is overlooked. It is present in everyday general practice when the doctor prescribes a placebo, a medicine or pill that has no therapeutic value, with the instructions, 'There is nothing to worry about. Take this three times a day, and you will find you are soon better.' And although the medication is a worthless substance the patient obtains relief. The force can also be seen in the patient who goes to a sympathetic doctor and feels better after talking to him, and before taking any medication.

A more striking example was presented by a doctor during a BBC television programme a few years ago. He told the viewers how he, as a young anaesthetist, had become enthusiastic about the use of hypnosis in medical practice, and after being in attendance at two unsuccessful operations to graft skin on a man who was covered from head to foot in warts, asked the consultant for permission to try and remove the warts by hypnotic suggestion.

Permission was granted and as the hypnotic sessions progressed the patient's skin, over the entire body, became clear. The young doctor received a shock when he proudly presented the cured patient to his senior colleague, for only then was he told that he had created medical history, because what he assumed to have been warts was an incurable ailment only resembling them.

From that moment onwards the anaesthetist tried to treat the same condition on many occasions. He used the same method of inducing hypnosis, and identical suggestions, but further success eluded him.

Why did the treatment work when the doctor knew he could cure it, but had no effect once he knew the condition was incurable? There was no answer to that question, and therefore the x factor – the element involved in the cure – remained an enigma.

There have been many attempts to try and explain away this phenomenon, the most popular being 'it is all in the mind', which implies that the therapist contributes nothing, and the patient can cure himself. It is because of this attitude that people say to the person who is suffering from stress disorders, 'Pull yourself together', and consider it to be a weakness of character. But is there more to it than mind over matter?

In 1970 Dr Yannic Guéguen of Basle, Switzerland, tackled this knotty problem and wrote that the answer lay in 'the doctor's healing power'. According to him, when the patient elects to go and see a doctor he trusts about his complaint, the first step in the healing process has been made. At that point the patient has unconsciously decided, 'I know the doctor has the power to make me better.' This belief is subsequently confirmed when talking to the physician, and reaffirmed when taking the medicine prescribed.[1]

Guéguen claims this is at the root of the cures obtained by unorthodox healers. The unregistered practitioner believes in his ability to heal, but the people who visit him have even more faith that he will be able to help them, and it is their faith which frees

[1] See 'The Doctor's Healing Power' in the Documenta Geigy publication *Beyond Belief*, published by Geigy (UK) Ltd., Pharmaceutical Division, Macclesfield, Cheshire, 1970.

the natural healing capacity within the organism to combat the illness.

To be fair to Dr Guéguen, he also wrote for the benefit of his colleagues, that expertise and up-to-date knowledge of medical advances is not sufficient if the doctor is going to fulfil his professional role adequately. He emphasizes that they should be aware that the interview is more than just a time to collect clinical data about the patient's condition, and see it as an opportunity for the patient to talk about himself and receive from the medical healer the understanding no one else has been able to give him. Doctors may have forgotten the importance of the point Guéguen makes, but patients have not. Hence their preference for one doctor over another. 'I don't want to see Dr Blank,' they tell their friends, or the receptionist if they have the courage, 'he never seems to be interested.'

The consequences of the doctor's attitude were related by Dr M. M. Ernst, a general practitioner and psychoanalyst, as he described the case of a thirty-year-old married woman with one child who was suffering from depression.

She was seen by a psychiatrist who made careful and accurate notes, then wrote her a prescription for two different types of pills, two hundred of them in all. Upon her return home the patient was still depressed, and swallowed most of the pills she had been given. Fortunately she survived the massive overdose, but told her own doctor, after leaving hospital, that while the psychiatrist was nice to her, she had the feeling he did not understand her problem and that made her feel so isolated that she took the pills. Her own physician listened to her attentively, and as the patient talked she revealed what lay behind her depression and attempted suicide.[2] Although Dr Guéguen's explanation, and the corroboration, is interesting it tends to verify the 'mind over matter' theory, and leaves much unanswered.

Back in August 1971 a reporter from the Sunday newspaper, the *News of the World* came to interview me, and he, Jack Shepherd, wrote a piece entitled, 'Having a Baby can Upset Dad':

[2] Dr M. M. Ernst, 'The Importance of Empathy', *General Practitioner*, 23 May 1969.

When our three children were born I suffered with a single, painful boil for each of them – on my fingers for the boys and on my thighs for the girl.

For months each boil resisted all attempts to remove it. But once I had visited the maternity home and seen mother and child safe and well I went home and recovered swiftly. The last time this happened was seventeen years ago. And I've never had a boil since.

To me (and to countless other expectant fathers with similar inexplicable ailments) those boils and the three scars I still carry have always been a source of amusement. . . .[3]

In his story the x factor was at work again, but how and why?

An American psychologist, Harry Stack Sullivan, who died in 1949, put forward the theory that there exists, particularly between mother and child, a presently unknown biological means of non-verbal communication which he called 'empathy', and to Sullivan it was through this 'emotional contagion and communion' that the infant first acquires feelings of anxiety. If the mother is anxious she transmits her feelings, biologically, to her baby, and the infant's body duplicates what she is feeling.

There is a mass of empirical evidence to support this hypothesis. The Revd Dr Michael Wilson, MD, MRCP, a Research Fellow in Theology at Birmingham University provided a typical example. He quoted a woman who had a cancerous breast removed and then received a letter from the hospital informing her that the results of a recent check-up were unsatisfactory, and she would have to be re-admitted.

She did not tell any member of her family about the letter, but her four-year-old son followed her around the house all that morning and would not let her out of his sight. At lunch time, and without any warning, he burst into tears, clung to her skirt, and said, 'Don't go back into hospital, Mummy.'[4]

It is argued that incidents like this are not proof of empathy, and it is feasible that the mother had emitted non-verbal 'distress' signals, which her son, having been separated from her earlier when she went into hospital for the mastectomy, had

[3] Issue dated 15 August 1971.
[4] The Revd Dr Michael Wilson, 'Communicating a Bad Prognosis', *General Practitioner*, 3 December 1971.

picked up and fortuitously interpreted as being related to hospital.

However the same argument cannot be applied to the findings of Martha McClintock of Harvard University Psychology Department who conducted research to try and ascertain why best friends, and girls living together in a college dormitory, tended to menstruate at the same time. In the same way that mothers and daughters, or sisters, who live together in a house where there is no man tend to synchronize their periods.

Studying 135 girls, McClintock, having eliminated all possible variables, came to a tentative conclusion that their bodies communicated and re-emphasized their mental friendship by physically menstruating at the same time.

Like many psychologists who advance a new concept Harry Stack Sullivan did not try to prove the existence of empathy by a scientifically designed research programme. This was left to a fellow American, Mr Cleve Backster, a lie-detector expert whose Backster Zone polygraph procedure is the standard technique employed at the US Army Polygraph School and by numerous Police Departments, and a former interrogation expert with the Central Intelligence Agency. In other words Mr Backster is a man whose evidence cannot easily be dismissed.

His work began by accident in the morning of 2 February 1966, when he was watering a plant in the office, and he idly speculated if he could measure how long it would take for the water to rise up from the roots of the plant, and reach the leaves.

He attached a psychogalvanic reflex (PGR) electrode to each side of a leaf of a Draena Massangeana plant with a rubber band, and lined up his instruments.

Instead of the recording needle on the chart going up as the water level rose in the plant, it went down, and the only time Backster had seen that happen before was in a human being experiencing emotional stimulation. That brought about his decision to treat the plant as human and to apply the threat-to-well-being principle, an accepted procedure to trigger off emotional responses in men and women.

Backster dipped one of the leaves into a hot cup of coffee, but there was no measurable reaction. He tried music, but the needle remained static. Feeling slightly frustrated he thought, 'I'll burn the damn thing', and although his threat was only *thought* the polygraph recording needle leapt upwards, registering alarm. It was a breakthrough, so he got some matches and made a few passes at the plant with a lighted match. The needle recorded extreme agitation.

Having established that thoughts alone were sufficient to bring about a plant reaction, Backster ruminated, if the experiment was repeatable with similar results it would tend to indicate that there existed an undefined primary perception in plant life. For months afterwards he used a variety of plants and they all reacted to any unusual thoughts or activity around them.

For instance, when his Doberman Pincher dog entered the room where the plants were being examined, the needle went up, and Backster tells how the plant knew when the dog was anxious and prowling about. In the room where his dog slept there was an electronic timing device which was linked to a loud alarm, and five seconds before the alarm rang off it was preceded by a barely audible click. The dog did not like the noise of the alarm, and when he heard the click he would get off his bed and leave the room. Backster in a different room with his plants always knew when the dog commenced his anxious roaming even though he, Backster, could not hear the pre-alarm click, because the plant wired up would immediately register the Doberman's anxiety.

What was transpiring was strange to Cleve Backster, and he contacted Professor J. B. Rhine, formerly at Duke University, and then head of the Foundation For Research on the Nature of Man at Durham, North Carolina, and the world's foremost authority on extra-sensory perception.

Rhine was not too helpful, and suggested that psychokinesis – the ability of the mind to affect people or move objects by thought – might be involved, and it was possible that Backster was unconsciously influencing the plants, and the recording needle by his own thoughts.

Although he was annoyed by Rhine's assessment, it made Backster aware of the need to conduct future experiments in a manner that obviated human influence. He purchased some brine shrimp, normally used as live food for tropical fish, and decided to see what effect the suffering of other species had upon his plants.

When the brine shrimp were killed by dropping them into boiling water, the polygraph needle leapt upwards in a surge of frenzied anxiety. As he watched a new concept was forced upon the experimenter, 'Could it be that, when cell life dies, the cell emits a signal which other cells can pick up?'

To test that hypothesis Backster had to eliminate the human element completely by installing complex, but reliable equipment. He obtained mechanized shrimp-dropping trays, a complex electronic randomizer, a programmer circuitry, multiple PGR monitors, and linked them all together so that the tests could be programmed and carried out without human involvement. At random times unknown to Backster live shrimps were dumped into boiling water, and still the plants registered distress.[5]

Since those early days Cleve Backster has come up with additional findings. He has conditioned plants in a traditional Pavlovian way, by giving them an electric shock, and discovered that he only has to think about administering a shock, and they would go into a coma like a person fainting. Moreover, an interesting fact to emerge was that the plants only reacted anxiously to the death of healthy brine shrimp. When sickly and dying specimens were dropped into boiling water their death was ignored.

Nor is the communication with his plants confined to shrimps. Any violent action against any living cells produces similar results. The scraping of blood from an accidental wound, treating an open wound with a strong antiseptic, or breaking an egg. And Backster told a journalist how he decided to have a yogurt for lunch one day, and as he stirred the contents of the carton the recording needle nearly shot off the graph paper!

The person who destroys a living plant in the presence of those plants wired to his instruments, will also evoke an anxiety

[5] Full details of the early experiments are contained in a reprint entitled *Evidence of a Primary Perception in Plant Life* by Cleve Backster, originally published in the *International Journal of Parapsychology*, Vol. X, No. 4, winter, 1968.

reaction whenever he or she re-enters the room. In addition to registering anxiety the plants also register what Backster sees as the equivalent of pleasure. The leaves of a plant reared by one person show they are closely attuned to the grower, and when Backster thought about returning to his office while he was in New Jersey – fifteen miles away and separated by the Hudson river – he noted the exact time on his stop-watch. Upon his return he checked the needle-record of the plants he had raised, and the graph recorded a pleasurable reaction at that exact moment.

Backster is now convinced that this perception is to be found in all living cells; in the amoeba, the paramecium, other single cell organisms, mould cultures, yeast and even spermatozoa. But what type of energy is involved to facilitate the communication remains unknown. It is not electricity as we know it because Backster has tried to hamper the communication by using a Faraday screen and lead-lined containers which prevent the passage of electrical current, but they did not prevent the communication.

What Cleve Backster has done, and is doing has far-reaching implications. His experimentation provides an explanation to the power of prayer, and the work done in the 1950s at the Religious Research Foundation in Los Angeles, directed by the Revd Dr Franklin Loehr.

The Loehr group planted lima bean seeds, obtained from the same source, in two separate growing trays containing the same soil composite. The seeds received identical treatment, with the exception that one tray had prayers said over them.

The plants which were prayed for grew to a height of fifteen inches, while the beans which were nourished, but had no prayers said for them, had not even broken through the top-soil.

To eliminate the element of chance the same experiment was repeated, but instead of prayers being offered for strong growth, one tray of bean seeds was watered with water which had been blessed, while the other tray had water drawn from the same source, but was not blessed. The beans irrigated with blessed water grew at a faster rate than the control seeds.[6]

[6] A report on the Loehr experiments was published in *The People*, issue dated 4 January 1959.

In Britain, Brother Mandus, a Divine Healer of the World Healing Fellowship in Blackpool, Lancashire, repeated the experiments, as did Mr William Higgs of Levens, Scotland, and both had confirmatory results.

Dr Bernard Grad, a biologist at McGill University in Montreal conducted a series of controlled experiments with water which was in a sealed flask, and had been held by a psychic healer. When the water was used to irrigate barley seeds the seeds grew faster than the control group seeds which were given ordinary water. And Grad showed that if a depressed psychiatric patient held the water initially, and then it was given to the seeds, the growth rate was hampered.[7]

In their encyclopaedic *Psychic Discoveries Behind the Iron Curtain*, the authors, Sheila Ostrander and Lynn Schroeder, quote a conversation with the Russian psychologist, Dr Pavel Naumov, about an experiment where a litter of baby rabbits was taken aboard a submarine, and when it was submerged, i.e. when no communication was possible, the young rabbits were killed, one at a time. Back in the laboratory ashore, the mother rabbit had electrodes sunk into her brain, and at the moment her babies were killed she reacted.[8]

The effect of humans upon animals has been substantiated in Britain, and particularly in relation to milk-cows. Under controlled conditions a good stockman with empathy can increase the milk-yield by an impressive number of gallons, and if he is moved to another herd with identical grazing, fodder and care, but with a lower milk yield, the amount of milk his old herd produced will decline to the norm, and his new herd will produce more.

The same x factor exists in the relationship between cows and men responsible for artificial insemination. In 1971 I was asked to give a talk to a local section of the Artificial Insemination Department of the Milk Marketing Board, and afterwards, as we were having a drink the manager told me how some of his men had

[7] 'Some Biological Effects of the Laying On of Hands: A Review of Experiments with Animals and Plants', *The Journal of the American Psychic Research Society*, April 1965.
[8] Prentice-Hall, Inc., New Jersey, USA, 1970, pages 31-3.

a consistently high conception rate, while others were always low.

He said he had tried everything in an attempt to isolate what was happening. The men with a high conception rate were transferred to areas where the conception rate had been consistently low, and the men with a low rate had been moved into a high rate area. It did not make a scrap of difference. Before long the conception rate in the formerly low rate areas mounted, and the high rate slipped.

'We have tried bringing the men with a low conception rate back into the training school,' the manager said, 'and then gone out with them to supervise, and to ensure they are doing the job properly. There is no doubt that they are using the same spermatozoa and technique as their successful colleagues, but there is that "something" lacking in them.'

Sitting with us was a young man whose conception rate had been continually high. He had listened to what his boss had to say, and he added, 'I think it all depends upon whether you like the job you are doing, and like your cows. If you don't like them, why should the beasts conceive?'

To me, the words of the artificial inseminator showed that H. S. Sullivan was correct when he said that empathy was a biological communication between humans. But his breadth of vision was limited, and he did not take his concept far enough, because the research of Backster, Loehr, Mandus, Grad, Higgs, and others has shown there is a form of contact between all living organisms, and once this is understood the so-called mystery of the healing process disappears.

As the son of a famous lay hypnotist, Henry Blythe, I was horrified by the way he treated his clients, because he was not interested in trying to assist them to understand why they had their symptoms. Far from it. He ignored all the principles of established psychotherapy.

When his clients arrived at his consulting rooms in Gloucester or Torquay he would listen to them talking about their problems for a few minutes, and then he would induce hypnosis. While they were in the state he would tell them, in a convincing, authoritative way, that all their symptoms had gone, and from that moment onwards they would be well.

I remember we were out taking a walk together when I tackled him about his unorthodox methods, and he told me, 'Peter, I am not interested in all the psychological theories you talk about. They are fine for you son, if you believe in them. But to me they are rubbish. I'm not a hypnotist like these doctor friends of yours who rely upon suggestion. I am a mesmerist, and I believe, like Mesmer, that all around us is an unseen energy field, and there are some people who can tap the energy and use it. You can feel the energy in your body when you are properly attuned to it, and once you have captured it and you touch your client they go out like a light. You don't hypnotize them. It happens, just like that.' (He snapped his fingers.) 'They are mesmerized.'

Because I was not aware at the time of Backster and the others, and in any case the conversation took place before the experiments were set up, what he said sounded like voodoo mumbo-jumbo, and as Henry is an intelligent man I tried to make him see how unscientific his ideas were.

'OK Dad,' I said in a tone which I realized later must have been patronizing, 'but how do you know what is wrong with your client, and how do you know how to proceed, and what to say to them while they are in hypnosis – sorry, when they are mesmerized?'

Unperturbed he answered,' When you have the power in your body you know what the client needs. He doesn't have to tell you anything. And, in any case, it is the energy which flows out of you and into him which cures. The words, which come to you like a "zing" from outer-space, are what he needs to hear, but they only supplement the energy which really frees him from his symptom.'

Then I did not understand him. We were talking a different language, so I diplomatically tried to change the conversation. Henry must have sensed (?) this because he added, 'Son, you may not like what I believe. You may think it is rubbish. But this you cannot escape from – the fact that it works.'

And it does work for him. Contrary to all the rules, his success rate is high. His clients remain free from all their sympto-matology for life in some cases, and for many, many years in others, and the number of times he sees them is far less than any psychodynamically oriented hypnotherapist.

But here let me add a few words of warning. I still believe, and with good reason, that hypnotherapy and psychotherapy should be a combination of empathy and analysis.

Having added that personal comment we may proceed further. In the light of the additional knowledge quoted above I can now appreciate that Henry's technique has a lot in common with the work being done by faith, spiritual, divine and all the other healers, although I am not too sure Henry and the healers I have bracketed him with will be pleased with the comparison.

Today it is estimated that more than a million people in Britain every year go to healers, and Elizabeth Anstice who quoted these figures in her article 'A Question of Faith',[9] questioned why they seek unorthodox help. Her answer was, 'Presumably either because they are, indeed, healed, or because a healer can give them something which they fail to get from an orthodox doctor.'

Possibly the mechanistic training a doctor receives prevents him from utilizing the x factor of biological empathy in his treatment, but when members of the medical profession are asked why and how healers effect cures the stock reply is, 'because the conditions are psychosomatic'.

Mr Harry Edwards, a spiritual healer, and President of the National Federation of Spiritual Healers which has more than 2,000 healer-members, admits that many of the conditions he treats are psychosomatic, but by no means all. And he sees the renewed interest in spiritual healing as being due to the negative outlook of many doctors who tell their patients there is no hope for recovery, or 'there is nothing more that I can do. You will have to learn to live with it.'

Yet, the healers' work remains wrapped up in metaphysical mysticism as it has been for centuries, and when it is suggested that the time has come to make a scientific investigation into how it is effective there is opposition.

In a recent monograph entitled 'Comments on Research into

[9] *World Medicine*, 1 December 1971.

Spiritual Healing',[10] Mr Edwards opposes research into the part played by the healer in the healing process on the grounds that the healer is passive, and only an agency for the wiser intelligence emanating from the spirits of dead healers such as Louis Pasteur and Lord Joseph Lister. Part of his argument against research is based upon the fact that the healer does not have to be told what the illness is, for the spirits in their wisdom already know and they direct the hands of the healer, and the healing energy, to the afflicted spot.

This line of reasoning is wide open to doubt, for as the reader has seen from Martha McClintock there appears to be a non-verbal body-to-body communication, and towards the end of the last century it was a common occurrence for so-called 'good hypnotic subjects' to be put into a deep state of hypnosis, and told he or she would be able to inform the hypnotist what a patient was suffering from. The hypnotic subject would be instructed to touch the patient, a period of cogitating silence would follow, then a verbal diagnosis would be forthcoming, and while the hypnotized person had no knowledge of medicine, when the patient was examined by a physician the diagnosis was found to be correct.

As guidance from the spirit world of the dead was not involved in the hypnotic diagnosis it cannot be categorically claimed by anyone that spirit aid is essential to the healer. Of course, if there is a life after death, and sensitive people can communicate with those who have ceased to inhabit the material earth, it is possible they can help in the way Mr Edwards postulates. Where I take issue with him is because he does not recognize there might be another explanation, and only by conducting research into the part played by the healer in the healing process can the truth be ascertained.

In another section of his paper Mr Edwards remarks upon the feeling of heat which is felt by both healer and patient when the hand, or hands, of the healer locates the diseased part of the body. This, he says, is noticeable:

[10] January 1972. Obtainable from The Sanctuary, Burrows Lea, Shere, Guildford, Surrey.

... where there is a healing purpose of a special character, such as healing of rheumatism, arthritis, fibrositis, inflammations and with some internal maladies. While this heat force is felt by both healer and patient, it is not physical heat. If a thermometer is placed between the healer's hand and the patient, there is no increased recording of temperature.

By referring again to the book *Psychic Discoveries Behind the Iron Curtain* by Ostrander and Schroeder, a book which has become a standard reference for anyone involved in the energy phenomenon, we find the Russians have also noticed the healing heat Mr Edwards wrote about.

Sheila Ostrander and Lynn Schroeder devote considerable space to the work of Semyon and Valentina Kirlian who have developed a photographic process which allows the energy residing in all living organisms to be captured on a photographic plate.

According to the authors the Kirlian method was used to test a well-known Russian healer, a retired army officer, Colonel Alexei Krivorotov, who works in conjunction with his son who is medically qualified, because Krivorotov and his patients felt the healing heat, but there was no temperature change. The Kirlians took photographs of the Colonel's hands as he was working and there was a definite change of energy emission. Normally there were small flares of energy coming from all parts of the hands, but when Krivorotov was healing, and the patient felt the heat most intensely, the overall emissions died down and were replaced by one strong, focussed beam.[11]

The Russian healer agrees with his British counterpart, Mr Edwards, in believing the energy he channels into his patients to cure them comes from a source outside himself, but the Kirlian photographs tend to offer a different explanation.

As the energy was already present within the Colonel, and the photographic plates show it was and is in all living matter, then it is possible that all he did was unconsciously to mobilize it into one strong, unified healing force.

Irrespective of who is correct it is undeniable that **healing does**

[11] *Psychic Discoveries Behind the Iron Curtain*, pages 218–20.

take place. I was present at the National Federation of Spiritual Healers 'Healing Day' in Manchester on 29 April 1972, and had the opportunity of seeing Harry Edwards healing, of talking to him afterwards, and talking to many other prominent spiritual healers.

Although I was, and still am, sceptical about the spiritual dogma attached to their form of healing, I and a British doctor who was present as an observer saw Edwards call for arthritic and rheumatic sufferers to join him on the platform, free their bound lesions (albeit temporarily), and move their limbs without displaying any signs of discomfort. When this demonstration was completed he urged those he had helped to continue seeing a spiritual healer in their vicinity for treatment, to ensure that the improvement he had obtained became permanent.

At the Manchester meeting I talked to Colonel Marcus McCausland, the founder of the Health for a New Era organization which is investigating on an international level all fringe therapies, and encouraging research to discover if the results the fringe therapists obtain are solely due to suggestion, or through presently unrecognized principles. He told me that the reason for his attendance was to obtain the opinions of the spiritual healers so he could formulate what they considered to be the laws of healing.

The foundation he heads has now published a preliminary paper. There is agreement amongst them that illness is a blockage of the free flow of energy at one or more levels, i.e. the physical, emotional, etc, and the document then defines how the healers see themselves being able to effect cures.

Under Point 4 it reads:

... the healer harmonizes himself with the patient and with the natural energies which he will be channelling to the patient at all levels. It is helpful, but not essential, if the patient is relaxed and expectant.

5 *Belief and source* The healer has a complete belief in the ability he has been given to act as a channel for the natural or divine energies which are always available at all levels.

6 *Attitudes* The healer works with sympathy, faith and hope for the patient and his problems. ...

8 *Healing* Through guidance and intuition the healer removes the *causes* of the disease by cutting out the energy blockages at whatever level they exist; then sufficient energy is channelled for that occasion so as to permit the many energy levels of the patient to start or complete the healing process. The healing session may take place with the patient in the presence of the healer, or with the patient at a distance from the healer.[12]

9 *Time* Healing may be instantaneous or may be a slow process spread over a long period of time, with many visits to the healer. . . .[13]

This is couched in what many people will consider to be esoteric language, and I have quoted it, not to advertise any form of unorthodox therapy – there has to be considerable research before that – but to show that the art of healing is not confined to the acquisition of medical knowledge, and keeping up to date with the latest drugs. And to inform the registered medical practitioner who cannot admit he has healing powers invested in him that he is encouraging his patients to look to unregistered practitioners who allow, and encourage, empathy to exist as a part of their treatment.

[12] The reader is reminded how Backster's plants were, apparently, in thought communication with him over a distance of fifteen miles.
[13] A copy of the full text is available from Health for the New Era, 1a Addison Crescent, London, W14 8JP.

Chapter 11
Human energy: fact or fiction?

It is common practice for people to refer to human energy in their everyday conversations as if it actually existed: 'I simply haven't got the energy to do anything,' 'He is a bundle of energy, and always on the go,' 'What I need is a tonic to pep me up, and give me some energy.' These are only a few examples of how we sum up our feelings, and although they may be unscientific they explain what we think is happening to us.

If we take a patient who is suffering from depression and apply the anxiety=tension=stress formula we can understand how energy is dissipated. At the outset the patient becomes anxious and the body responds by becoming tense and ready for action. To maintain his state of physical tension the patient calls upon his reserves of energy. If the anxiety-tension is not relieved within a comparatively short period of time and he enters the stress-stage it is not long before his reservoir of energy is completely depleted. From then on he has a feeling of emptiness. Everything, even thinking, becomes too much of an effort, and he is depressed.

Exactly the same thing happens to the insomniac. Being unable to recharge his energy system during sleep he finds, by mid-morning, he has hardly any energy left, and has to force himself to complete whatever tasks have to be done during the remainder of the day.

In his earlier years Sigmund Freud made a study of psychic energy which he believed circulated throughout the body and according to his hypothetical construct, if the life force (libido) flowed freely, the person remained healthy. However, if it was impeded, then the energy would collect in the blocked region, and transform itself into any of a variety of pathological conditions. Of course what Freud proposed was not new. The wheels of history had turned another full circle, because his psychic energy was a modernized version of what the sixteenth-century physician and alchemist, Paracelsus, called Munis, and two centuries later Franz Anton Mesmer referred to as 'animal magnetism'.

But it was after Freud cast aside his libido theory for the more acceptable, and less dangerous, concept of ego anxiety that experimental investigations were carried out by Wilhelm Reich to ascertain if there was evidence of its existence. Reich proved, at least to his own satisfaction and that of those Reichians who have duplicated his experiments, that bio-energy is a fact. Following further experimentation over a considerable number of years Reich announced he had proved that bio-energy was only a part of a cosmic, orgone energy which is all around us and fills the universe.

In the same way that many of Freud's associates objected to his libido theory, many of Reich's friends and colleagues refused to accept his findings, and while they were not prepared to duplicate his experiments to check their validity, they launched into a personal attack to the effect that he had ceased to be an objective scientist and had become a mystic. Worse still, when Reich refused to recant, they branded him as psychotic.

Today most members of the medical profession talk about energy, but tend to dismiss it when asked to consider its medical implications. It was because of this attitude I found myself asking the question, 'Is human energy a proven medical fact, or nothing but a part of our folk lore inheritance?' For a long time there was not even a glimmer of an answer forthcoming, until coincidence presented me with a variety of interesting 'facts'. To start at the beginning. It was in the summer of 1971 that I laid out a research programme for this book, and I thought I should include in it a section devoted to the Chinese branch of medicine, acupuncture, because it seemed, from what I had read, a method of treating psychosomatic diseases which was becoming more popular in Britain, and therefore pertinent.

At this point I should inform the reader what I then thought about acupuncture. I was sure that the secret of its success lay in discomfort. That a patient having had a number of needles stuck into him was bound to feel better once they were taken out. As for the theory, about which I knew nothing, I saw acupuncture as a legacy of ancient, mystical medicine, which based its treatment on the idea that all illness was caused by evil spirits invading the body, and before recovery was possible the devils had to be let out, in this case by the small punctures made in the skin by acupuncture needles.

Loaded with these prejudices I visited the founder and President of the Acupuncture Association in the United Kingdom, Mr Sydney Rose-Neil, FAcA, who gave me a lot of his time, and kindly provided me with a comprehensive report he had written in 1966 on the subject, together with a bundle of files.

The origins of acupuncture, according to the Acupuncture Association, go back 7,000 years when Chinese physicians noted that soldiers who were wounded by arrows sometimes recovered from an illness of long-standing. They continued to observe and evolved the theory that, if the skin was penetrated at certain places, a number of diseases were apparently cured. With the passing of time the Chinese doctors saw that the size of the incision was unimportant. It was the exact location and depth which brought about a remission, so they began to copy the effects of the arrows by artificially puncturing the skin.[1]

As an introduction to a scientific method of medical treatment it failed to impress me, and when I later read, 'Conditions which can be successfully treated include migraine, headaches, ulcers and digestive troubles, lumbago, arthritis, fibrositis, sciatica, rheumatism, dermatitis, eczema, psoriasis and other skin conditions, high blood pressure, depressions and anxiety states, asthma and bronchitis and many others . . .'[2] I was positive the therapy was valueless, and hocus-pocus from beginning to end, because those illnesses were the acknowledged stress-disorders.

But I continued to read:

The theory behind acupuncture is that there exists in the body a dual flow of energy called Yin and Yang. These are expressed in everything

[1] *The Register and Directory of Members*, published by the Acupuncture Association.
[2] Ibid., page 3.

in the universe, day and night, elasticity and contractability, hot and cold, life and death, etc. Everything has its force of opposition, but this opposition by its very existence is itself complementary. Yang tends to stimulate, to expand and is the positive principle, while Yin tends to sedate, to contract and is the negative principle.

Health is dependent on the equilibrium of these two forces, firstly within the body and secondly within the entire universe. They must be protected and kept in equilibrium, for otherwise disease will develop.

The Chinese discovered that this 'vital energy' (Yin and Yang) circulates in the body along the 'meridians' similarly to the blood, nerve and lymphatic circuits. The flow along the meridians may be detected by electronic and other means. These paths of vital energy (Ch'i) disappear at death.

There are fourteen main circuits which are known as meridians, each associated with a different function or organ. The state of these meridians can be assessed at the two radial pulses felt on the forearm just above the wrist. The condition of Yin and Yang and the state of the various systems in the body can be estimated before the illness develops. Traditionally, the Chinese doctor was only paid a fee when the patient was well. It was, therefore, in his interests to keep the patient well and thereby receive his remuneration.

The body keeps Yin and Yang in harmony by dispelling surplus energy via the skin surface at certain points on the meridians, and by shifting energy to deficient areas of the organism. Traditionally there are about eight hundred of these points, but the existence of new ones is continuously being found. In diseased conditions there is a breakdown of this process and the energy flows are unbalanced. Often certain of the points become painful when pressed, and these are associated with the condition which is developing. In order to treat the illness it is necessary to rectify any imbalance in the energy flow. By piercing the skin at certain points the energy flow is stimulated or sedated. . . .'[3]

This did nothing to alter my attitude, but it was interesting that the energy theory was cropping up again under the Chinese names of Ch'i, and Yin and Yang. All it did was to give rise to a series of questions.

What is the medical profession's attitude towards acupuncture? Had it been successfully used to treat organic illnesses as opposed to the psychosomatic ones already listed? Could the

[3] Ibid., page 4.

acupuncturists prove the existence of the energy flow, and if so, how did they do it?

Taking each question in turn I discovered a British Medical Acupuncture Association, but it has few members, and is a definite minority group.

From press-cuttings I saw in December 1962, in the issue of *Family Doctor* a reader asked, 'What is acupuncture . . . and particularly has it any real value in cases of rheumatism?' The answer given was, 'Do you really think that this sort of hooey is likely to help your rheumatism in any way?'

Dr John Anthony Parr answering questions put by readers of the magazine *Annabel* wrote, in his column 'The Doctor Replies', 'Such treatment cannot cure anything. But if you are capable of intense self-deception then such treatment can bring relief if no disease is present . . .'[4]

Again this was not encouraging, so I began looking at its use in organic diseases, and began to find things which could not be explained away by the mind-over-matter, or psychosomatic theory.

In 1968 the founder of the Medical Acupuncture Association, Dr Felix Mann, read a paper at Cheltenham saying he had become attracted to the potentials in the art of Chinese medicine in Strasbourg where a case of appendicitis was apparently cured by acupuncture.[5]

What he said was confirmed by an earlier issue of the *Chinese Medical Journal*.[6] 116 cases of acute appendicitis were treated with acupuncture, and 92.5 per cent recovered within an average of six days without undergoing surgery.

At a Canton school for 250 deaf-mute children an Army medical team had been working for three years, and a group of visiting Western journalists were told 80 per cent obtained some degree of hearing, while others recovered completely and were able to live normal lives. A minimum of six months' treatment was needed to recover partial hearing, but some of the deaf mutes required up to two years, and the spokesman said certain types

[4] Issue dated July 1970.
[5] Reported in the *British Medical Journal*, 2 November 1968.
[6] 'Acupuncture in the Treatment of Acute Appendicitis', February 1960.

of deafness caused by meningitis and the side-effects of the drug streptomycin did not respond as well.[7]

The longer I looked, the more I discovered. In Tientsin, a large industrial port on China's north-east coast, doctors announced that they had used acupuncture to cure cancer of the liver, and the treatment had also been successful in cases of blindness, deafness, and paralysis caused by polio.[8] Then the big news came out of China, supported by eye-witnesses, television films and photographs, that acupuncture was being used as the sole anaesthetic agency for operations of all kinds, ranging from brain to open-heart and abdominal surgery. This created tremendous interest and a storm of controversy in the medical world.

The US Surgeon General's office in Washington DC, announced this year that a full scale investigation is to be made into acupuncture; more than one thousand doctors turned up to hear a lecture on it out on the West Coast of the USA and here, in Britain, the College of Acupuncture which normally has a preponderance of unregistered practitioners like osteopaths, etc, as students is receiving an increasing number of applications from physicians.

But there are those who cannot accept that acupuncture has any value, and are suggesting that acupuncture anaesthesia is a fraud, and only a form of hypnosis.

Because I have conducted training courses for doctors and dentists throughout the British Isles I have been inundated with queries, asking if acupuncture is hypnotism.

I know that in the last century Dr Esdaile was performing major and minor surgery under hypnosis; that open-heart surgery is currently being performed under hypno-anaesthesia; and that hypnosis is being widely used to assist women in childbirth. But the acupuncturists have demonstrated that good results have been achieved with patients in a coma; that rabbits and cats have responded, and in France there is an association of acupuncture-veterinarians.

Equally I am aware that there is a type of animal hypnosis which I saw demonstrated in New York City in 1970, at the

[7] *South China Morning Post*, Hong Kong, 14 May 1971.
[8] *Natal Daily News* of South Africa, 4 May 1971.

annual Convention of the Association to Advance Ethical Hypnosis, but there is no evidence whatsoever to show that the catatonic state induced in them has a direct therapeutic value.

In view of all this I have been forced to conclude that acupuncture is not comparable with hypnosis, and that suggestion plays a minimal, if any, part in the effects produced by Chinese traditional medicine. And to a large extent this assessment was borne out when, as recently as August 1972, I interviewed Mr Ian Urquhart, who has spent the last seven years in Japan investigating acupuncture with Dr Manaka.

He told me about the 'Manaka two metal contact' control of pain where no verbal suggestion is involved. Taking a pain-location on a limb they would put a small piece of copper near to the pain location, and a small piece of iron at a distance from it. Then, upon application of pressure the pain subsided, but by merely reversing the positions of the iron and copper, the pain returned. They repeated this procedure many times and both Dr Manaka and Mr Urquhart agreed it indicated the presence of an energy that can be controlled and altered by metal contact. As to the nature of the energy, they could only conclude that it showed some aspects of being a magnetic force.

Another interesting experiment the two of them carried out, details of which were subsequently published in an American medical journal, was based upon the extra-ordinary acupuncture meridians which approximate a figure 8 in the body. They would take an area of pain and insert two needles, connected by ordinary electrical wire with a transistor inserted in it to make a unidirectional flow of current, along the figure 8 extra-ordinary meridians, with the pain area between them, and the pain subsided, or returned, dependent upon which way the transistor allowed the current to flow.

At the Manaka hospital they experimented with a woman suffering from a third degree burn covering the shoulder and part of the breast. After covering the badly burned section with tinfoil they inserted a needle in the opposite leg to the burn, in a Yang meridian, and connected it, via the lead, to the tinfoil. The patient had a good night's sleep without requiring any sedation, and the following morning the exudation had dried.

The two of them, using certain acupuncture points, have treated patients with anaemia, and within twenty-four hours the condition was rectified. Mr Urquhart said, 'This is a fact, and any laboratory can confirm that we can do it.'

He also told me about Dr Nakatani in Japan who has a cure-rate for colour-blindness of approximately 90 per cent. In the West this is considered to be a congenital condition and irreversible. Doctors say it may decrease, but it will always remain. Urquhart stressed the importance of this in Japan where people suffering from colour-blindness are barred from having a driving licence, and are unable to enter the medical profession.

By the time I sat down to write this book I had altered my views on acupuncture, and was reluctantly ready to accept that there was more to it than simply letting evil spirits out of the body through the holes caused by acupuncture needles. But the final question remains to be answered, 'Have they proved the existence of their Yin-Yang energy flow, and if so how?'

The North Korean professor, Kim Bong Han, together with a team of researchers at the Kyungrak Research Institute in Pyongyang, commenced looking into the traditional school of medicine known as Dongeuihak, or the Kyungrak part of it, because he believed that modern medicine, and biology, had failed to adequately explain the unity of the organism. While exploring that avenue he discovered the physical existence of the meridians as a separate physiological system. He further showed that the energy circuits contain DNA and RNA – the two substances basic to life and reproduction – and his carefully documented work, together with histological, pathological and photographic evidence is now available in the English language.[9]

In 1950 French acupuncturists developed an electronic instrument, based upon the Wheatstone bridge, which demonstrated the existence of the acupuncture points. As an electrode was passed over the skin of the body a magic eye lit up at each of the eight hundred points where the energy leaves the body.

[9] See *Report at Symposium*, Pyongyang, 30 November 1963. Also *Kyungrak System and Theory of Sanal*, published by the Medical Science Press, Pyongyang, 1965.

Five years later the Germans brought out a more sophisticated instrument, and in 1960 Mr Rose-Neil developed it further. Now acupuncture instrumentation is being used in Russia, Japan, and throughout Europe.

The Japanese and Russians claim that their latest energy-detecting instruments can tell what part of the body is deficient in energy, pinpointing exactly where the free-flow is blocked and can detect illnesses before any pathology and symptomatology appears.

In Russia, the Kirlians saw on their photographic plates that there were specific spots on the body where the discharge of energy was greater than elsewhere. This did not mean much to them until they met a surgeon, Dr Mikhail Kuzmich Gaikin, who was interested in acupuncture, and he was able to confirm they were the places the ancient Chinese had delineated as acupuncture points.[10]

Whether this is sufficient evidence to prove the existence of human energy must be left to the individual, until further research is completed. But a growing number of people are accepting it, like Dr David J. Sussman of Buenos Aires, President of the Argentine Acupuncture Association, who said at the Second World Congress of Acupuncture held in Paris, in May 1969:

What makes us occupy ourselves with Reich in a Congress of Acupuncture is the notable fact that the energy discovered by Reich has many points of contact with the energy of the Chinese, the former having over the latter the advantage of a clearer scientific formulation. . . . In the orgone energy discovered by Reich we see the actual and scientific version of the Yin-Yang energy. . . .[11]

[10] *Psychic Discoveries Behind the Iron Curtain*, pages 222–8.
[11] Dr D. J. Sussman, 'Medical Acupuncture and Bio-Energy', *Character and Energy*, Vol. 3, No. 3, September 1972.

Chapter 12
Pills, patients and people

The discovery of cellular pathology by Rudolf Virchow in the nineteenth century and his formulation that all illnesses are really diseases of the cells, together with Louis Pasteur's work showing that infections are caused by germs, and Robert Koch's detection of the tubercle bacillus causing tuberculosis, has resulted in doctors being trained along the same lines as mechanical engineers.

This becomes apparent when a patient visits his medical practitioner with a particular physical symptom, because the doctor sees his task in the same light as a motor mechanic who tackles a car brought into the garage with a fault. The mechanic listens to the owner's description of what is wrong with the vehicle, listens to the engine, and then, if he is lucky, diagnoses the malfunctioning part, after which he will prescribe a remedy, the medicine. Of course if the condition is too serious he will put on his overalls and become the surgeon, getting deep inside the engine, removing the ailing part, repairing it, and re-assembling everything so that it is in running order again.

To continue the comparison a little further, if the mechanic decides the fault is outside his sphere of competence, he will refer the patient, the car, to one of the many specialists available, perhaps an electric-automotive engineer.

Without wishing to minimize this technical expertise of the medical profession, the strides made in pharmacology, immunology, surgical techniques such as transplants, the utilization of advances in mechanical technology which have given us the iron lung, the kidney machine, etc, what is surprising is that they continue to ignore the question, 'Why do some people succumb to an infection or a disease, while others exposed to the same environment remain immune?'

This unanswered question is most important. The fact that it is disregarded indicates the symptoms are considered to be more important than the person who is ill.

Robert Koch may have discovered the tubercle bacillus which infects the lungs, causing TB, but tuberculosis has long been acknowledged by a large number of reputable doctors as a psychosomatic condition, and that certain people, through their psychological make-up, react to stress by producing this disease. Moreover, prior to the discovery of penicillin by Sir Alexander Fleming, the standard treatment was to remove the sick person from his normal, stress-provoking environment (this was also a prophylactic measure to prevent others of a similar disposition from being infected), and provide complete rest, plenty of fresh air and sunshine.

Nowadays the diseased lungs are treated via the mechanical approach of antibiotics and the patient's mental attitudes are overshadowed by the treatment. However, one cannot blame the doctors for this. Their medical training, together with the prevailing mechanistic attitude, has conditioned them into accepting a depersonalized doctor-patient relationship, and caused the unintentional abuse of drugs by the overworked general practitioner. In Britain this state of affairs has been exacerbated by the heavy demands placed upon GPs operating inside the National Health Service.

At a seminar on hypnosis I was holding in Cheltenham a few years ago, a GP in a large group practice told me that he had so many patients to see at each surgery that, 'I use what I call IPD.'

Intrigued, as I was meant to be, I asked him what the initials meant.

'Instant possibility diagnosis,' he replied. 'My partners and I have worked it out that we have approximately two-and-a-half minutes to give each patient. Therefore as one of them comes through the door I have my pen poised over the prescription pad, and as the patient is telling me what is wrong with him I make an instant possibility diagnosis. I write out the script, and tell him, "Take these as directed, and if you don't feel better next week come back and see me again."'

Let me make it quite clear, the doctor did not like having to function that way, but as he said, 'There is no alternative, and thanks to my training and experience most of the time my IPD is accurate.'

This lack of contact time has alienated people from their doctors and the breach between them is being widened by the increase in group medical practices. Formerly a person knew the doctor, and more important, the doctor knew the person, and there was a rapport between them. But this is disappearing. A patient now makes an appointment when he feels ill, and as there are three doctors in the group he has no way of knowing which of them he is going to see until the receptionist informs him, 'Will you go into that room. Doctor Blank will see you now.'

Admittedly the doctor has the patient's case-history card before him, but a piece of paper is a poor substitute for personal knowledge of the person's background, and it can also be misleading.

One overworked doctor did not know the person sitting in front of him, he only had his record card, and from that he deduced the man was a chronic hypochondriac. Therefore, when the man started to complain about his stomach ache, a pet complaint of his, the practitioner wrote out a repeat prescription for an innocuous bottle of medicine. The patient left, but in the early hours of the following morning he was admitted to hospital with an acute appendicitis. A mistake like that may not happen often, yet if that isolated incident is multiplied by the number of times doctors are forced into similar situations, it represents a potentially serious hazard.

To relieve the burden of the overworked GP a campaign has been instituted through the aegis of the news-media asking people to refrain from telephoning the doctor unless a house call is imperative.

In Britain this is a good idea because the welfare state has encouraged the attitude, 'I'm paying for the National Health Service, so I don't see why he shouldn't come and see me at home. It is what I am entitled to.' But the more conscientious members of the public have taken it to heart. After experiencing the sterility of visiting the doctor's office, and being urged not to ask him to visit them at home, they have taken to prescribing self-medication.

In the United States there is the identical phenomenon, but for an entirely different reason: the extortionate medical bills.

The dangers involved in this development of self-treatment were voiced at a Royal Society of Health Conference held in Eastbourne in 1969 by Mr J. P. Kerr, chairman of the practice committee of the Pharmaceutical Society of Great Britain, when he told delegates of a survey conducted with five hundred pharmacists. It was discovered that a rheumatic patient was taking a hundred aspirins a week without realizing there were any dangers involved in what he was doing. A mother wanted to dose her six-month-old baby with a full-strength aspirin, and another mother wanted to give her little girl a dose of laxatives because the child was 'doubled up with pain' – she had an appendicitis!

Mr Kerr also said that a number of people were unaware of the constituents of the drug they were taking and frequently gave themselves a double-dose by taking one preparation for a headache, and another for a stomach ailment.

The dangers of over-prescribing are not, however, confined to the general public. The same is true of the profession, and rather than dwell upon the well-publicized examples of depressives' becoming addicted to amphetamines which give them a boost, insomniacs' becoming dependent upon sleeping pills which occasionally leads to an overdose and death, I would draw attention to another facet which is not so patently obvious.

To clarify the point I am trying to make it is necessary to leave the ranks of orthodox, registered medical practitioners and look at the unregistered practitioners in Britain; the acupuncturists, herbalists, naturopaths, osteopaths, lay-hypnotists, and healers of all descriptions who are usually lumped together and categorized as 'quacks'.[1]

(Actually the use of the term is amusing when its origins are appreciated. Not all that long ago in the annals of medical history

[1] In the USA Federal and State Laws restrict the practice of medicine, in most forms, to those who have qualified at recognized universities, and there is not the diversity of unregistered practitioners that we have in the United Kingdom.

our doctors were largely naturopathic-herbalists. Then chemo-therapy started to make its presence felt, and particularly in the treatment of syphilis. A group of doctors in Germany decided to break away from the traditional approach, and treat those who had caught the venereal disease non-naturopathically; by giving them mercury – quicksilver – which in the German language is *Quecksilber*, the first part of the word being almost identical to the German word used to describe the meaningless noises – the quacks – of ducks and geese. It was those physicians who pre-scribed a substance alien to the organism, the forerunners of to-day's orthodox medical practitioners, who were called 'quacks'!)

The 'healers' are generally attacked by orthodox hardliners, because the doctors fear that the training of the unregistered practitioner is either inadequate or non-existent, and that especi-ally the lay-psychotherapist and lay-hypnotist may be placing their clients at risk by treating a symptom rather than its cause, which could result in symptom-transference, with the client developing an even more serious maladjustment. While this attack has some validity, because psychotherapists have seen that a client suffering from stress-symptomatology may temporarily surrender a psychosomatic condition and replace it with a psy-chological one, it is mainly spurious. For the registered medical practitioner is not adequately trained either, as medical schools do not devote any part of their curriculum to a depth study of psycho-dynamics. Therefore the trained doctor is more likely to treat the symptom rather than the cause than the lay-therapist as the latter cannot prescribe drugs.

By taking a brief look at a person with a high temperature I hope the picture will become clear. All practitioners agree that the body has within it natural, recuperative powers, and that all treatment, irrespective of what it is, should be aimed at assisting nature to effect the cure.

Dr Walter B. Cannon, a famous Harvard physiologist, did a lot of work in this area and showed how the body always tries to return to a state of well-being through an internal, homoeostatic process. When a body is infected by a virus the homoeostatic defences are activated. Anti-bodies are produced to kill the in-vaders as quickly as possible, and to restore normal functioning.

Another method is to raise the body-temperature to a level where the aliens cannot survive. But what happens when we get a high temperature? We are given drugs to lower the body-heat, and there is now the strong possibility that, by using drugs indiscriminately in this way, the body does not return to complete homoeostatic good health, but slowly becomes more and more prone to disease, because it has not had the chance to work through the illnesses naturally.

Before the fury mounts and I am attacked from all sides, let me put on record that I am in favour of drugs when and where they save lives. What I am saying is, that medical practitioners, as a result of their training and through *necessity* (lack of time, etc), tend to use drugs in cases where they are not absolutely necessary, and their continual use can upset the natural resistance mechanisms.

I arrived at this radical conclusion through giving a lecture in London on hypno-analysis. I told the audience that, contrary to popular belief, it was a rare occurrence for a prevailing symptomatology to remiss when a client had consciously recalled and understood the event which had triggered off the symptom. 'That is the myth of the "psychic abscess",' I said, and explained how it was necessary to probe further into the unconscious mind to locate the earlier episodes which had built up until the moment the symptom broke through.

'Only after the client has relived or recalled all the sensitizing events is he or she in a position to cope with life free from their complaint,' I concluded.[2]

At the end of the lecture, and when question time was over, a gentleman came up to me and said, 'Mr Blythe, are you interested in naturopathic medicine?'

As politely as I could I tried to tell him I wasn't, as I thought the nut-addicts were, to use a colloquialism, 'nuts'. He took my lack of interest in his stride. 'Well I think it would pay you to look into it, because you will find that people who go to naturopathic practitioners regress through their previous illnesses, in the same way your clients in analysis do.'

[2] For full details see the chapters on hypno-analysis and hypno-diagnosis in my book *Hypnotism: Its Power and Practice*.

Before I had time to ask him for more information he merged into the people leaving the hall. But I did not forget what he told me, and when I met Mr Sydney Rose-Neil who, in addition to being President of the Acupuncture Association, is one of the country's foremost authorities on naturopathic medicine, and Director of Tyringham Naturopathic Clinic, I asked him about it.

We were sitting beside the open air swimming pool at the clinic when I broached the subject, and Mr Rose-Neil appeared somewhat surprised at my ignorance, but patiently explained,

When we put our patients on to a fast, and then an individually prepared diet, they often do regress. They regress backwards through illnesses they have had, right through childhood, and although the reappearance of the symptoms is not as prolonged as the original sickness, the symptoms are there and recognizable. If you have not got a full case history, and this happens, it can be alarming when you see the symptoms, because in some cases they are severe.

For instance, if a person has had scarlet fever as a child, their body can throw up all the physical signs of scarlet fever. Fortunately the naturopath has been taught to expect this regression to happen occasionally, and it is after their regression we consider the body is ready to start functioning properly. So you can see your informant was correct. Whether you like it or not, there is a direct comparison between your clients regressing in analysis and people undergoing naturopathic treatment, as far as regression is concerned.

Our conversation was an eye-opener to me, but when I thought more about it I remembered catching malaria while in Ceylon, and the doctor giving me quinine. And that was not a fever-suppressant – its value lay in the way it promoted the fever-crisis!

It would be to the reader's disadvantage if he concluded from what I have just written that doctors are unaware of the dilemma. Many are aware, and there are suggestions appearing regularly in the medical press calling for a halt in massive drug prescription, and alterations in medical training to include psychotherapy. However, these suggestions are not easily implemented. The majority of people have been conditioned into expecting medication, and if they do not get it they feel cheated.

An example of this is the case of a man who recently caught a stomach virus and telephoned the doctor to visit him at home. When the doctor arrived it was suggested to the man that if he stayed in bed and kept warm everything would be fine in a couple of days.

'Aren't you going to give me something for it?' the man asked.

The doctor countered his question with a question, 'Why? Don't you think you will get better if I don't give you something?'

The man was very unhappy. He thought the doctor was being off-hand and failing in his duty, and he let the doctor know this. So, in the end, and against his better judgement, the doctor wrote out a prescription. My only hope is that it was a placebo, but I doubt it!

On the medical training side, a leading member of the British Medical Association who personally wants to see the human touch restored to medical practice, and the whole person being considered instead of just the symptom, was asked why psychotherapy and psychodynamics was not an integral part of the medical training curriculum. He answered to the effect that medical students had insufficient experience of people to benefit from a knowledge of psychotherapy, and after they had graduated, with six or seven years of learning behind them, they felt they did not need to know any more and in any case they were far too busy.

If we accept his view it does not alter the fact that people want to talk to their doctor. They want to be treated as people and not patients; to know what is wrong with them, and not be fobbed off with platitudes or non-answers.

In 1972, at a British Psychological Society conference held in Nottingham, Miss Margaret Sloan called upon psychiatrists to bridge the gulf between them and the people they were treating, by talking about themselves, giving intimate details of their life-style, instead of remaining silent and aloof. She also suggested that the intimacy include a frank discussion of mutual sex problems.

Miss Sloan was only echoing Dr David Hawkins, Professor of Psychiatry at the University of Virginia, when he told hundreds of doctors attending the 1969 meeting of the American Medical

Association's symposium on sex education, 'I say it is your duty as physicians to ask a patient directly about his sex problems, instead of sitting back and hoping the subject will never arise.'

I asked an American physician in New York City if he thought the time was coming when his colleagues would become more interested in the psychogenic aspects of people's problems, and his reply was far from encouraging.

Both the public and the profession may want the over-prescribing of drugs to be replaced by understanding. That is how it should be, but you have to consider the position of the doctor.

He may know why a woman has her asthma. She has a domineering husband who cannot tolerate any show of emotion on her part. So, what does the doctor do? Does he tell the wife, your husband is causing your asthma, so that she can go home and tell him? Boy, if that were to happen the man would be round at the office ready to knock the living daylights out of the doctor. Or does he tell her that her husband needs treatment, and until he gets it she is going to continue having her asthma? Now that may be true, as we both know, but he'll still get his head knocked off.

Faced with those alternatives it is far better to give her a new inhaler and her pills, because the doctor has enough problems on his hands without creating fresh ones.

But, if you really want an honest answer, I'll give it to you. The medical profession will only become interested in the practice of psychosomatic medicine when the general public begins to realize that pills are for patients, those who are sick and need them, and not for people with problems.

Chapter 13
A look into the future

An internationally known and respected figure in the world of psychotherapy said that psychology is a science, and its object is to study human behaviour in order to be in a position to predict, with some degree of accuracy, how a person will react in the future in a given situation. Psychotherapy, he continued, was the art of understanding what lay behind the individual's overt behavioural patterns, so the therapist can help the person to effect changes in the personality.

By taking his definition of psychology and relating it to the material presented in the preceding chapters of this book we can predict and outline those measures necessary to combat the spread of the stress-disease plague without being accused of indulging in clairvoyance.

However before any changes can be implemented an alteration of the curriculum in medical schools is a pre-requisite, and in addition to medical students receiving adequate training in psycho-dynamics and psychosomatic medicine, a part of their time will have to be devoted to their own sex education.

It is all very well for progressive educationists and physicians to suggest that sex education should be taught to school children, but it cannot stop there, because as a member of the panel of the American Medical Association's symposium on sex education in 1969 said, doctors belong to a group which 'is grievously ignorant and rather prudish in matters of human sexuality'.

Their ignorance has been apparent when people have gone to see their doctor to discuss a sexual problem, only to be told, in the kindest way, 'It is quite common, so don't worry about it,' 'These things happen, and there is not much we can do about it,' or the complete, unintended rejection, 'This isn't really my province, but if you like I will make an appointment for you to see a psychiatrist.'

These answers to lack of female orgasm, premature ejaculation and inability to obtain a penile erection are not due to lack of interest, they are the result of the doctor's lack of training in this stress-producing area of human relations.

But if we leave sex to one side, there are signs that a slight breeze of change is already blowing through the medical profession.

In Britain, at King's College Hospital in London the Faith Courtauld Research Unit has been established to 'carry out research into the broader aspects of cancer':

The aim of the Faith Courtauld Unit is to study the problem of cancer as it affects the individual as a complete human being. Thus the studies will begin with an examination of the stresses of life which may be involved in the development of the disease. The work will lead on to the impact which the experience of the disease has on the individual and his or her resulting attitude to life, family, work and recreation. These findings are being backed up by parallel studies of body chemistry and of the body's ability to fight the disease.

The studies which have already started are being made by a multi-disciplinary team including pathologists, physicians, psychiatrists and surgeons. At present the unit is concentrating on the study of cancer of the breast in women, but it is hoped to extend the study to other forms of cancer, as funds permit. . . . [1]

Meanwhile out on the West Coast of the United States, the Esalen Institute, one of the main centres for 'third force' psychotherapy, has announced that it is to run a three-year course in San Francisco for medical personnel called 'Program in Humanistic Medicine'. The planned schedule is intensive, and is to include among other things, various techniques 'to teach personnel to be more fully aware of the personal and inter-personal dynamics of the medical situation . . .'. There is a section on preventive medicine, 'such as meditation, inner-imagery, bio-feedback and others to effectively deal with stress

[1] A leaflet published by the Courtauld Research Committee, King's College Hospital, Denmark Hill, London, 15 December 1971.

. . .'. Another on psychosomatic medicine, nutrition, and unconventional medicine, and included in the latter is to be 'Chinese medicine, acupuncture, herbal medicine, psychic healing, yogic therapy and manipulative therapy', because Esalen believes these 'could serve as valuable inputs to Western medicine'.[2]

Superficially the Esalen project looks as if it will form a bridge between the past, the present and the future in medicine. But when it is carefully analysed it can be seen that it places a greater burden upon the medical practitioner by asking him to be all things to all men. Whereas all the things mentioned may have a place in the future of medicine there is no reason why one person should be expected to do everything.

In Germany there are naturopathic physicians and acupuncturists functioning within the Health Service and alongside their orthodox colleagues, and the same is true in China where traditional medicine works side by side with modern medicine.

To ease the burden on the doctor the future will see the emergence of a new medical auxiliary which I have tentatively called the 'medical counsellor'.

The medical counsellor will be trained in counselling techniques, individual psychotherapy and group therapies, and manipulative therapy, thereby ensuring people receive what they need, and not as at present, what the therapist has to offer them.

His or her role in the medical hierarchy will be a position between the general practitioner and the psychiatrist who is already badly overworked.

When a GP sees someone suffering from stress, instead of merely writing out a prescription for a specific drug, or referring them straight to a psychiatrist, he will ask them to have a talk to their medical counsellor. Using a reflective interview technique similar to Dr Leonard Cohen's, the counsellor will see the person for one, two or three sessions to ascertain the possible cause of the problem, then contact the GP with his observations and proposed line of therapy, if any is necessary.

The GP will maintain responsibility for the person–patient, and give the consent for the counsellor to proceed.

[2] Published by The Esalen Institute, 1776 Union Street, San Francisco, California, 94123.

'Will this cost a lot of money, and where will it come from?' is a question I have been faced with when outlining these proposals to medical friends. Part of the cost of the counsellors' salary will be defrayed by the money saved from present drug-expenditure, but the hidden financial benefits will accrue from industry, as it is hoped there will be a vast reduction in the millions of working days currently lost due to stress symptoms.

But, let us lift the veil on the future. Children will either be born at home or in small, pleasant maternity homes, far removed from the clinical atmosphere of a hospital, and mothers will be encouraged to have their babies with them at all times, providing the skin-to-skin contact the infant requires.

These more emotionally secure children will go to smaller schools, with a small number of children to each class, and they will be taught by teachers whose training will have included dynamic psychology to enable them to understand the needs of the individual children working with them. Every school irrespective of its size and the age of the children, will have a counsellor who may have been a teacher, but has no academic duties, and he or she will act as a buffer between the children and the academic staff.

When the young adult leaves school he or she will be encouraged to work in various parts of our industrial and business world before making a decision about future full-time employment.

The education authorities, and large business combines who employ vast numbers of people, will arrange courses in human communication. Their medical counsellors will use group and individual techniques so that people can give vent to their frustrations, break through their armouring, and work out any problems they have in a suitable, accepting environment.

Utopia?

Not a bit of it.

In the future people will still have problems, they will still feel anxiety at times, but they will be better prepared to cope with life and, far more important, they will not have to die prematurely.

Bibliography

Blythe, P., *Hypnotism: Its Power and Practice*, Arthur Barker, London, 1971.

Braaty, T., *Fundamentals of Psychoanalytic Technique*, Wiley, New York, 1954.

Brown, J. A. C., *Freud and the Post-Freudians*, Penguin Books, Harmondsworth, Middx., 1967.

Fenichel, O., and others, eds., *The Psychoanalytic Study of the Child*, International Universities Press, 1945.

Fisher, Sir R., *Smoking: The Cancer Controversy*, Oliver & Boyd, Edinburgh and London, 1959.

Groddeck, G., *The Unknown Self*, Vision Press, London, 1967.

Grossman, C. and S., *The Wild Analyst*, Barrie and Rockcliff, London, 1965.

Haugen, G. B., Dixon, H. H., and Dickel, H. A., *A Therapy for Anxiety Tension Reactions*, The Macmillan Company, New York, 1963.

Jackins, H., *The Human Side of Human Beings*, Rational Island Publishers, Seattle, Washington, USA.

Janov, A., *The Primal Scream*, Dell Publishing Co., New York, 1970.

Kent, C., *The Puzzled Body*, Vision Press, London, 1970.

Kinsey, A. C., *Sexual Behaviour in the Human Male* and *Sexual Behaviour in the Human Female*, W. B. Saunders Co. Ltd., London, 1948 and 1953.

Liss, J., *Co-operative Help: The Art of Helpful Listening*, 68 Queensway, London, W2.

Lowen, A., *Sex and Personality*, Institute of Bio-Energetics, New York, 1963.

Malinowski, B., *The Sexual Life of Savages in North-Western Melanesia*, Routledge & Kegan Paul Ltd., London, 1932, 1969.

Mouly, G., *Psychology for Effective Teaching*, Holt, Rhinehart & Winston, New York and London, 1968.

Murray, E. J., *Motivation and Emotion*, Prentice-Hall, Inc., New Jersey, USA, 1964.

Ostrander, S. and Schroeder, L., *Psychic Discoveries Behind the Iron Curtain*, Prentice-Hall, Inc., New Jersey, USA, 1970.

Pinney, R., *Creative Listening*, Creative Listening Ltd., Loddington, 1970.

Reich, I. O., *Wilhelm Reich*, Elek Books Ltd., London, 1969.

Reich, W., *Selected Writings*, Noonday Press, New York, 1961.

Reich, W. *Die Funktion des Orgasmus*, International Psychoanalytischer Verlag, Vienna, 1927. Available in English translation as *The Function of the Orgasm*, Panther Books Ltd., St Albans, Herts., 1968.

Reich, W., *Character Analysis*, Noonday Press, New York, 1967.

Selye, H., *The Stress of Life*, Longmans, Green & Co., London, 1957.

Index

Other Pan books that may interest you
are listed on the following pages

Folk Medicine 60p
D. C. Jarvis MD

The tough, hard-living mountain folk of the State of Vermont have a time-honoured folk medicine.

The late Dr Jarvis, a fifth-generation native of Vermont, lived and practised among these sturdy people for over fifty years. This book is the result of his deep study of their way of life and in particular of their concepts of diet. These he was able to test against his formal medical training and prove by long experience.

Here he offers a new theory on the treatment and prevention of a wide variety of ailments – the common cold, hay fever, arthritis, high blood pressure, chronic fatigue, overweight and many others – and holds out a promise of zestful good health for young and old.

Little wonder, then, that this absorbing book has proved immensely popular throughout Britain and America.

'There is not a family in the land who won't find its theories – and propositions – fascinating' DAILY EXPRESS

Not All in the Mind 60p
Dr Richard Mackarness

How unsuspected food allergy can affect your body and
your mind: a revolutionary approach to the modern
epidemics – allergies, headaches, lethargy, obesity, bowel
disturbances, depression and other mental illness

In this vitally important book, Dr Richard Mackarness,
doctor and psychiatrist, shows how millions may be made ill,
physically and mentally, by common foods such as milk,
eggs, coffee and white flour.

He relates case after case from his clinical practice where
patients with chronic ailments resistant to other methods of
treatment were cured by identifying and eliminating foods
to which they had developed unsuspected allergy. The
history and mechanics of this unique approach to ordinary
though disabling complaints are given in fascinating detail.

Dr Mackarness also describes how you and your doctor can
identify and cure your allergy by a simple method, without
drugs – before it is too late.

Selected bestsellers

- [ ] **Jaws** Peter Benchley 70p
- [ ] **Let Sleeping Vets Lie** James Herriot 60p
- [ ] **If Only They Could Talk** James Herriot 60p
- [ ] **It Shouldn't Happen to a Vet** James Herriot 60p
- [ ] **Vet in Harness** James Herriot 60p
- [ ] **Tinker Tailor Soldier Spy** John le Carré 60p
- [ ] **Alive: The Story of the Andes Survivors** (illus)
  Piers Paul Read 75p
- [ ] **Gone with the Wind** Margaret Mitchell £1.50
- [ ] **Mandingo** Kyle Onstott 75p
- [ ] **Shout at the Devil** Wilbur Smith 70p
- [ ] **Cashelmara** Susan Howatch £1.25
- [ ] **Hotel** Arthur Hailey 80p
- [ ] **The Tower** Richard Martin Stern 70p
  (filmed as *The Towering Inferno*)
- [ ] **Bonecrack** Dick Francis 60p
- [ ] **Jonathan Livingston Seagull** Richard Bach 80p
- [ ] **The Fifth Estate** Robin Moore 75p
- [ ] **Royal Flash** George MacDonald Fraser 60p
- [ ] **The Nonesuch** Georgette Heyer 60p
- [ ] **Murder Most Royal** Jean Plaidy 80p
- [ ] **The Grapes of Wrath** John Steinbeck 95p

All these books are available at your bookshop or newsagent;
or can be obtained direct from the publisher
Just tick the titles you want and fill in the form below
Prices quoted are applicable in UK

Pan Books, Cavaye Place, London SW10 9PG
Send purchase price plus 15p for the first book and 5p for each
additional book, to allow for postage and packing

Name (block letters)⎽⎽⎽

Address⎽⎽

⎽⎽

While every effort is made to keep prices low, it is sometimes
necessary to increase prices at short notice. Pan Books reserve the
right to show on covers new retail prices which may differ from
those advertised in the text or elsewhere